"So often our culture encourages us toward the quick-fix solution or shortcut to whatever it is we have our hearts set upon. But with the deep things of God, there's likely no drive-through version or fast-track approach. His ways are higher than ours—and they are often slower too. My friend Banning's brilliant book is such a timely reminder of how over time we can develop deep roots in Christ, and how these various roots then become the foundation for a life of lasting impact."

—MATT REDMAN, songwriter, UK

"So it's about time we have a book from Banning Liebscher, after his years of leading the Jesus Culture movement and gatherings of hundreds of thousands of young leaders around the world! Banning hits the jackpot with this new book on identity, purpose, and calling—a much-needed and timely message and a challenge for all leaders. *Rooted* reminds us that leaders must not only embrace the process of becoming who God has called us to be but actually love it too!"

—BRAD LOMENICK, past president of Catalyst and
author of *The Catalyst Leader* and *H3 Leadership*

"Banning takes us back to the basics in this brilliant, simple book. *Rooted* is a gift to an entire generation that could otherwise easily forget or, worse yet, never hear the foundations for a distinctive Christian life."

—GABE LYONS, Q founder and author of *Good Faith*

"This foundational concept of being rooted is so timely for our culture. Strong winds will come at us and want to take us in every direction, but only the trees that have deep roots will stand when these winds blow. It's our unseen self that truly is our strength. I highly recommend anyone to dig deep into these pages. Thank you, Banning, for such an important book for our days."

—CHRIS TOMLIN, singer and songwriter

"I've been doing life and ministry with Banning Liebscher for more than fifteen years. I've watched him live out the message that is his new book, *Rooted*. I've watched as Banning has continuously surrendered his life to God, devoted himself to prayer, served the Church, and intentionally moved toward relationships and challenges within community. He is certainly a leader who has stepped out in faith, allowing God to develop deep roots in his life. I have personally been challenged by Banning's uncompromising trust in God and commitment to being strongly rooted in Him. The message of *Rooted* is a timely and prophetic message this generation needs to hear. In an age where everything is so attainable and we are all encouraged to dream big, it is so important to understand the cost of what God calls us to. It's easy to dream and have vision, but to surrender our lives in trust to God and to allow Him to develop us from the inside out takes tremendous courage and strength. But it is possible and so incredibly important! If you are in it for the long haul, if you want to be able to sustain the dreams God has put in your heart, if you want to bear fruit that will last, this is the book for you!"

—KIM WALKER-SMITH, president of Jesus Culture
Music and Jesus Culture Publishing

"This book connects with my soul! Amidst the highs and lows of life, my heart longs to be grounded in Christ. To be rooted in His truths. To be reminded that before God can work through us, He must do a work in us."

—KYLE KORVER, professional basketball player
for the Atlanta Hawks

"Few men in our generation have shaped the songs we sing, the places we gather, and the spiritual atmospheres we encounter, like Banning. In his book *Rooted,* it's easy to see his gift for practical lifestyle leadership. Banning's words have a profound undercurrent to push you into developing spiritual integrity. Many of us are looking for a front-row seat to an honest and real conversation about what it's going to take to go the distance. *Rooted* is a resource you want to have close throughout the years. It's a must-read book!"

—HAVILAH CUNNINGTON, director of Moral Revolution
and founder of Truth to Table Ministries

"Few voices of this generation are qualified to both biblically and practically detail the process through which God roots us into our purposes. One of those voices is undoubtedly Banning's. In his new book *Rooted,* Banning expertly engages the slow-motion button and give us powerful step-by-step insight into how God develops us to be who He has willed for us to be! Great read!"

—CHRIS HILL, senior pastor of the Potter's House
of Denver

"In every generation a heart comes along that beats so loudly for God, the sound is heard around the world. Banning Liebscher possesses this kind of heart—a heart whose soil continues to be tilled, watered, tended, and tested by fire—producing lasting fruit that nourishes the nations. In his book *Rooted*, Banning takes the enormous fruit of his own life and puts it directly into the hands of each reader, practically walking you into a life so rooted in intimacy and wisdom, it can thrive in every season."

—CHRISTA BLACK GIFFORD, speaker, songwriter, and
author of *God Loves Ugly* and *Heart Made Whole*

"Banning is a general to modern generation. He has great insight into discipleship and raising up a generation. This book will impact and empower you to live a life of greatness. I thoroughly recommend this book to you."

—RUSSELL EVANS, founder and director
of Planetshakers

"Finding your identity in Christ is so important in today's world. *Rooted* gives you the fundamental skills to guide you into being fully grounded and established in Christ, producing fruit that lasts. This book shows us that when we are fully rooted in Christ, we are positioned to influence the world around us."

—LUKE RIDNOUR, thirteen-year NBA veteran

"*Rooted*, the latest book by Banning Liebscher, is both intensely practical and wonderfully profound. I've had the pleasure of watching Banning become what he has written about—a man deeply rooted, who bears much fruit. His life in God is rich and real. For this reason, God is using him to transform the lives of countless people around the world. Learning to embrace God's process in our lives brings us to a place of rest, where trust becomes a natural expression of our relationship with God. *Rooted* is sure to have great impact on all who read it."

—BILL JOHNSON, Bethel Church, Redding, California,
and author of *When Heaven Invades Earth* and
Defining Moments

"Everyone champions accomplishments, but not many people champion the journey. I love Banning's take on how to embrace the journey and trust God on your way to enduring fruit. This book will help you redefine what success looks like in your life. It will give you keys to help you lean into the Lord when you are in process or feel far from your destination. And you will find yourself getting built up and learn how to enjoy the different seasons of life."

—KELLY CLARK, Olympic gold and two-time bronze
medalist in snowboarding halfpipe

"In order to fully achieve all that God has called us to do in our life, we must know our God-viewed identity! I believe Banning does that in *Rooted* by taking us through David's life and showing us how engaging in high-trust intimate relationships with God and community will allow us to truly serve others in a way that people will see Jesus and be impacted by Him."

—JEREMY AFFELDT, retired Major League Baseball
pitcher, three-time World Series champion, and author
of *To Stir a Movement*

"Many Christians struggle with the illusion of choice, believing there are multiple paths to purpose and passion. In *Rooted,* Banning invites us on a journey down the narrow path that defines the process of becoming fruitful in our service to Christ. You will find this path to be both practical and biblical, one that defines terms like *serving, humility,* and *community.* A legacy is a history worth repeating; *Rooted* equips and encourages us to embrace our true calling, following Jesus and living a legacy that produces everlasting fruit."

—LYLE WELLS, author and speaker

BANNING LIEBSCHER

ROOTED

THE HIDDEN PLACES
WHERE GOD DEVELOPS YOU

WaterBrook
PRESS

Rooted
Published by WaterBrook Press
12265 Oracle Boulevard, Suite 200
Colorado Springs, Colorado 80921

Trade Paperback ISBN 978-1-60142-840-0
eBook ISBN 978-1-60142-841-7

Library of Congress Cataloging-in-Publication Data
Names: Liebscher, Banning, author.
Title: Rooted : the hidden places where God develops you / Banning Liebscher.
Description: First Edition. | Colorado Springs, Colorado : WaterBrook Press, 2016.
Identifiers: LCCN 2015038390| ISBN 9781601428400 | ISBN 9781601428417
   (electronic)
Subjects: LCSH: Spiritual formation. | Christianity—Influence. | Change—Religious
   aspects—Christianity. | Church and the world.
Classification: LCC BV4511 .L53 2016 | DDC 248.4—dc23 LC record available at
   http://lccn.loc.gov/2015038390

Printed in the United States of America
2016

10 9 8 7 6 5 4 3

*To the dreamers and leaders on this journey
at Jesus Culture Sacramento.*

*May your lives be rooted deeply in God's process,
and may you bear fruit that has lasting impact
in this city and the nations of the earth.*

Contents

Why the Rooted Last

He shall be like a tree
　Planted by the rivers of water,
　That brings forth its fruit in its season,
　Whose leaf also shall not wither;
And whatever he does shall prosper.

Psalm 1:3

D eep inside every follower of Jesus is a desire to have a visible, lasting impact in the world. This desire was born in us when we believed the gospel. We who have tasted "the power of God to salvation for everyone who believes" (Romans 1:16) not only want to see that power at work in our lives, but we want to see it working through us, bringing the life and hope of Jesus to a broken world.

This desire for lasting impact is not our idea; it is God's. In John 15, Jesus announced that He chose and appointed us to *bear fruit:*

> I am the vine; you are the branches. If you remain in me
> and I in you, you will bear much fruit; apart from me you
> can do nothing. . . . You did not choose me, but I chose
> you and appointed you so that you might go and bear
> fruit—fruit that will last. (verses 5, 16, NIV)

If you are a follower of Jesus, then your calling and destiny are to be fruitful. Fruit is not a bunch of spiritual or religious activities like going to church, reading your Bible, keeping the Ten Commandments, or even preaching the gospel. Fruit means that when people taste your life, you taste like Jesus. If you are fully grafted into Jesus, the vine, then He says your life should produce tangible results that make people say, "Now that is Christlike."

Not only are you chosen and appointed to produce fruit, but Jesus said you are chosen to produce *much* fruit, and not only much fruit, but *fruit that lasts.* There's a difference between *some* fruit and *much* fruit. God's plan for your life is not conservative. He's not satisfied with minimal results. He expects to see much, and you should too. How much do you think you can know Jesus and become like Him? How much do you think you can show Him to the world? He wants that for you and much more. He wants you to bear fruit beyond what you could ask or think.

There's also a difference between *much* fruit and fruit *that will last.* God isn't satisfied with temporary results. He's in the business of permanent change. He's not looking for a month, or a year or a decade, of you growing more like Jesus and pursuing the things He calls you to do. He's looking for a lifetime impact, a generational impact, and an eternal impact.

Abundant, enduring fruitfulness is the mandate on your life. Ultimately, enduring fruitfulness in your life and the rest of the body of Christ is the key to seeing nations transformed, cities impacted, and culture shaped. But abundant, enduring fruitfulness will only happen, Jesus says, if you "remain in" Him. What does that mean?

ROOTS BEFORE FRUIT

In the growth cycle of fruit-bearing plants, fruit comes at the very end. The cycle starts with a seed being planted in the ground. When watered, the seed will break open and begin to put down roots. That root system will continue to grow as the seed forms a shoot and eventually breaks through the surface of the soil into air and sunlight. Both the plant and its root system will keep growing until the plant is strong and mature enough to bear fruit. Significantly, in order for a plant to survive, much less bear fruit, its root system has to take up more space underground than the plant takes up above ground. When you look up at one of those immense redwoods in the Avenue of the Giants, for example, you're actually standing on root systems that are wider than those trees are tall. This is the principle of foundations. A foundation always has to be bigger than the thing it is supporting.

Fruitfulness in your life comes about through a similar process. God plants the seed of His word inside you (see Luke 8:11) and waters it with His Holy Spirit, bringing it to life. He begins to give you insight into who He created you to be *in* Him and what He is calling you to do *with* Him. He stirs up that desire in you to have a lasting impact in the world. And then He starts to build a *root system* for that seed in your heart, your internal world.

Your heart is your point of connection with Jesus—the place where you become rooted in your relationship with Him. He wants to develop His heart-to-heart connection with you to the point where you become fully united with Him, where you think like He thinks, want what He wants, speak like He speaks, and do what He does. This is what it means to remain in Him. Only when you remain in Him will you produce fruit that lasts.

For you to bear abundant, enduring fruit, God needs to make you bigger on the inside than you are on the outside. You have to let Him build your root system in secret before He leads you into making a visible impact in the world. In his book *Power Through Prayer,* E. M. Bounds, one of the foremost authors on prayer, said, "The man—God's man [and woman]—is made in the closet. His life and his profoundest convictions were born in his secret communion with God."

DAVID'S ROOT SYSTEM

If you study in Scripture those who had a lasting impact, you will find that God led them through a season of preparation. For Joseph, that season lasted about thirteen years. Moses had to spend forty years shepherding in the wilderness before he was ready to lead the Israelites out of Egypt. Jesus Himself spent thirty years preparing for His three years of ministry—the most impactful ministry in history.

Of all the people in the Bible who bore lasting fruit, however,

David is unique, not just because of his incredible legacy, but also because of the depth of insight the Bible gives us into how God established roots in David's life.

The highlights of David's legacy are so impressive that a whole book on them wouldn't do them justice. Within his lifetime, he ushered in the golden age of Israel and established a brand-new culture of worship in the nation. Beyond his lifetime, the blessing on David's throne affected God's dealings with every king of Israel and Judah who came after him. The promised Messiah, Jesus, is called the Son of David and sits on the throne of David (see Luke 1:32). The psalms David wrote became a central part of worship for Jews and, later, Christians. In other words, every day for thousands of years, millions of people around the world have quoted, prayed, meditated on, and worshiped God with David's words. Finally, David was a prototype of New Testament believers, particularly because of his unique intimacy with God and his understanding that God desired a pure heart more than "sacrifice and offering" (Psalm 40:6). Every person on the planet, especially every Christian, has been impacted by the life of David. He bore lasting fruit that continues to this day and will continue into eternity.

Yet we can trace all of that fruit back to a single moment, the moment in which God planted a seed in David's life. This moment took place when he was young—probably between ten and thirteen years old—and it was pretty dramatic. The prophet Samuel, who at that time in Israel was like Billy Graham, the president, and Bono all wrapped into one, showed up at David's house and announced that he had come to anoint the next king of Israel.

David's dad, Jesse, didn't even think to call David in from the field, because Jesse naturally assumed that his youngest could not be the one destined for kingship when David had far more suitable older brothers to fill the role. Samuel surveyed Jesse's tall, handsome sons and thought, *One of these has to be the king.* Yet one by one, each of David's seven brothers stood before Samuel, and the prophet heard the Lord say, "He's not the one."

In the midst of this selection process, the Lord spoke a word to Samuel that we often pull out and quote: "The LORD does not look at the things people look at. People look at the outward appearance, but the LORD looks at the heart" (1 Samuel 16:7, NIV). God was saying, "I'm looking for someone who will let Me grow him on the inside before I grow him on the outside." He didn't want another King Saul. Saul looked like a king, but he wasn't sufficiently rooted in God's heart to lead a nation in God's way. God wanted a man He could groom for the kingship from a young age, a man who would actually *last* in that role for a lifetime and establish the nation on a firm foundation of faithfulness to God.

None of Jesse's older sons had what God was looking for. So the prophet asked, "Did we miss anyone?" They reluctantly called their little brother in from the field, and when Samuel saw him, he said, "There's the king." He anointed David with oil, and the Holy Spirit came on David in power, watering the seed of God's word and causing it to grow (see verse 13).

From that point, God began to build David's roots—a journey we will be exploring in more detail throughout this book. Only when that journey was complete did God's word come true:

When all the elders of Israel had come to King David at
Hebron, the king made a covenant with them at Hebron
before the LORD, and they anointed David king over
Israel.

    David was thirty years old when he became king,
and he reigned forty years. (2 Samuel 5:3–4, NIV)

Thirty years old! You do the math. God took somewhere between seventeen and twenty years to build roots in David and get
him ready to bear visible fruit.

A PASSION FOR ROOTS

My early twenties were a season of seed planting in my life. At the
time, I was serving as youth pastor at Bethel Church in Redding,
California, where exciting things were happening. By the hundreds, people were coming to know God, coming back to God,
receiving healing of their hearts, minds, and bodies, and being
filled with incredible joy and hunger for more of Him. The environment seemed to stir and awaken people's hopes and dreams
for what God wanted to do in and through their lives. It showed
up in our sermons, our prayers, our worship songs, and our
conversations—everyone was catching a vision for something
God was calling them to do.

    I was no different. I dreamed about the impact I would have
on the world. Practically every minister who came through town
and preached at our church called me out in meetings to confirm
what God was calling me to do and pray things over me regarding

my future. It felt like I was being barraged with encouraging words from people about my destiny. It was both exhilarating and terrifying to grab hold of the vision God was building in my heart and say, "Yes, God! Let's do this!"

Funny enough, however, no one praying over me added, "By the way, it will be twenty years before you start to scratch the surface of the things I'm telling you about." I wouldn't have believed them if they had. I was passionate and committed. I thought I was ready to step into the vision and be fruitful!

I now recognize that what I thought was readiness was actually the Holy Spirit coming into my life to water the seeds that were being planted and causing them to start forming roots. The vision God put in my heart was, in fact, to serve and equip believers to impact cities and nations for the kingdom. I wanted to be part of leading a generation to make Jesus famous and to shift our culture by putting His love and truth on display. The problem was that I did not yet understand what lasting impact was or how God brings it about. I hadn't really discovered the biblical model for how God prepares us for fruitfulness. When I read the stories of Abraham, Joseph, David, and other great saints, as well as Jesus Himself, and saw how long it took them to get where they were going, I thought, *Twenty years? You've got to be kidding me!*

Thankfully, both for my sake and the sake of those I was leading and equipping as a pastor, God shifted my perspective and showed me how critical it is for Him to build us on the inside first. The more I studied, observed, and experienced, the more it became clear to me that lasting fruit only comes through the long journey of putting our roots down deep in Jesus. Without deep roots, there is no fruit, and if there is fruit, it's not the kind that lasts.

My passion for roots has especially grown from watching what happens to people who are rootless. Jesus described them in the parable of the sower:

> But the ones on the rock are those who, when they hear, receive the word with joy; and these have no root, who believe for a while and in time of temptation fall away. Now the ones that fell among thorns are those who, when they have heard, go out and are choked with cares, riches, and pleasures of life, and bring no fruit to maturity. (Luke 8:13–14)

These people initially received the word with joy. They had a sense of excitement and anticipation for the vision God had planted in their hearts. Yet they did not allow the Gardener to come in and remove the rocks and weeds from the soil of their hearts. They did not allow Him to cultivate roots in their lives, and as a result, the word either died off or never bore any lasting fruit.

In the last twenty years, my position as a leader has grown from youth pastor to director of a worship-conference movement (Jesus Culture) to lead pastor of a church (Jesus Culture Sacramento). In these roles I have had the privilege of interacting with so many people who are trying to navigate their journeys of growth in God. I can tell you that as a pastor, nothing is more heartbreaking than watching the seed of passion and vision either die off or be strangled in people who were once running hard after God. Sadly, I have watched many Christians over the years fall into compromise, give up on their calling, or walk away from God entirely because they never allowed Him to make their internal world a place where His word could thrive.

On the other hand, nothing is more thrilling and satisfying than watching people who choose to yield, to embrace the journey of learning to remain in Christ and let Him establish their root system in secret. There is something truly supernatural about these people and what comes out of their lives. They taste like Jesus.

REDEFINING SUCCESS

When I was in my teens and twenties, I was amazed when people set out to run after their dreams or pursue a call from God. I celebrated their passion and faith to step out and risk everything for Him. Don't get me wrong. I still celebrate those moments and cheer people on as they start running their race. But I no longer have the same sense of awe and anticipation in those moments because I've realized something.

Anybody can start a race.

The real question over our lives is not how strong we will begin our race to pursue God's call but how strong we will finish it. There are far fewer finishers out there than beginners. Finishers are *impressive.* Why? Because they see what so many don't see: God's version of success is infinitely superior to the world's version of success.

God's version of success looks like building our lives on eternal things for eternal things. Anything less does not impress Him and shouldn't impress us. Unfortunately, many believers today don't live with forty years in mind, let alone eternity. One of my deepest concerns with the church is how hung up we have become with short-term successes that don't impress God one bit. We measure our success only by numbers—numbers that measure popularity and material success. People are looking at things like numbers of Twitter followers, Facebook likes, book sales, conference attendees, or warm bodies in the pews on Sunday morning as signs of success. While these numbers may show us some aspects of the impact we are having, they can't be our only measure of success.

Along with measuring success by short-term results, we are also measuring our significance by appearances, that is, the visible highlights of lives we see on social-media posts. If there was ever a more unstable source upon which to establish our significance, it's comparing our lives to others', especially through the images we see on Facebook and Instagram. Looking at someone's life through moments captured in photographs is like looking at an iceberg from the deck of the *Titanic*. You really have no idea what you're seeing because only a small part is visible. I know this because I'm fully aware that my social-media posts are all highlights. I post when my kids look adorable holding ice-cream cones or when the room is full of people at a conference I'm leading, not when I'm trying not to scream at my kids because they won't go to bed or when half the seats at the conference are empty.

To be clear, there's nothing wrong with our desire for significance, but there's everything wrong with where we are looking to define our significance. Similarly, there's nothing wrong with our desire for success, but there is a lot wrong with how we are defining and measuring success. Much of the church is looking in the direction exactly opposite to where we are supposed to be fixing our gaze:

> We look not at the things which are seen, but at the
> things which are not seen; for the things which are seen
> are temporal, but the things which are not seen are eternal.
> (2 Corinthians 4:18, NASB)

Neither appearances nor short-term success impress God. He looks at the heart, and He is looking for fruit that lasts. When we stand before Him at the end of our lives, the only thing that will matter is whether our hearts were aligned with His and we have long-term fruit. We want to live in such a way that we will hear Him say, "Well done, good and faithful servant!" (Matthew 25:21, 23, NIV). That's the success that must motivate us to embrace His process of building roots in our lives.

TRUST AND THE THREE SOILS

I am passionate about calling and equipping believers to embrace and thrive in God's root-building process. The purpose of this book is to look at Scripture and learn what to expect as God works to establish deep roots in you. I want to do all I can to eliminate the confusion and anxiety over why things in your life don't look the way you think they should look and to free you in the knowledge that you are right where you're supposed to be. I want to set you up to recognize and work with God as He builds you so that you don't resist Him.

As we journey together through this book, we are going to study the life of David and look at the different elements God developed in his root system during nearly two decades of process and preparation. The main thing God wanted David to be rooted in was a deep trust in Him. For God to establish this abiding trust in David's life, He had to prepare him in three different *soils*.

The first soil is the *soil of intimacy*. As a shepherd in the field, David built a relationship with God in prayer and worship, and dependence on God as he fought private battles with lions and bears. In the field, David developed a secret-place lifestyle.

The second soil is the *soil of serving*. As he served his father, brothers, and King Saul, David took a posture of humility that positioned him to receive God's grace. In serving, David chose to trust God to promote him rather than take matters into his own hands and try to fulfill the word on his life through self-promotion.

The third soil is the *soil of community*. When four hundred men joined David in the cave of Adullam, he learned what it meant to be a leader of men. He learned to trust his friends and brothers as well as God, learned to encourage and inspire, learned to take hits, learned to model a standard of honor, and learned to lead with a vision.

Each of these soils provided different but equally necessary ingredients to develop and strengthen David's root system of trust in God. After twenty years of being planted in these soils, David had a root system ready to sustain the weight of God's bringing to pass the calling on his life. Because David trusted God, God could trust David with a nation.

If David needed to be planted in these three soils, so do you. But the good news is that you don't really need to go anywhere to find these soils. God didn't anoint David and then say, "Let's get you to the castle and then you can start growing." He started the process right where David was and got him to where he needed to be. In the same way, you are where you are because God has planted you there. God can grow roots of trust in you at whatever job you have, at home raising children or preaching to the masses in India. He already has you positioned to find the soils of intimacy, serving, and community right where you are. Even if you have missed past opportunities, or if you have wandered far from God, you can start over right now, wherever you are, to let God begin to cultivate in you the strong root system He wants you to have.

God always develops us before He develops our vision. If we don't understand this, we will resist Him, get frustrated, and ultimately end up disappointed and disillusioned. But if we expect and embrace God's root-building process in our lives, guess what? We will not only set ourselves up for future success, but we will set ourselves up to thrive in that process. So let's embrace the process. We can't afford to settle for the lure of short-term success or a moment of popularity. Let's choose to be finishers. Let's choose to be those who are rooted.

2

Thriving in the Process

You will show me the path of life;
In Your presence is fullness of joy;
At Your right hand are pleasures
forevermore.

Psalm 16:11

I f you choose to embrace God's process and time line for building your root system, I believe it's possible not only to survive but
to *thrive* in the midst of it. By thriving I mean growing in wisdom, character, faith, endurance, strength, and more. Growing
isn't always comfortable, but it's exhilarating and rewarding.

The apostle Paul is an example of someone who thrived and
grew through every circumstance. We all know that he said, "I
can do all things through Christ who strengthens me" (Philippians 4:13). It's one of our favorite verses. It's on bumper stickers,
bookmarks, and tattoos. But we often forget the previous two
verses:

> Not that I speak in regard to need, for I have learned in
> whatever state I am, to be content: I know how to be
> abased, and I know how to abound. Everywhere and in
> all things I have learned both to be full and to be hungry,
> both to abound and to suffer need. (verses 11–12)

When we put "I can do all things through Christ who strengthens me" in context, we see that Paul was saying, "I've had seasons in life where I've had nothing and seasons where I've had everything. I've developed the ability to thrive in both seasons by learning to access the resource that never changes, no matter the season, namely, Christ's strength."

Similarly, when you read the Psalms, you find David spoke about all kinds of circumstances, ranging from celebratory to terrifying. He wrestled with impossibilities, fear, heartbreak, disappointment, betrayal, anger, and grief. But every time, the wrestling drove him back to the source of his strength: God. And every time David accessed that strength, whether in the field, a house, a cave, or a castle, it led to his thriving.

For us to navigate the same range of circumstances and find God, our strength in every situation, we have to know where to look and how to continue to look there in the face of the Enemy's distractions. Typically, these distractions are going to try to get us to (1) wish we were in someone else's process, (2) resist the lessons God is trying to teach us in our circumstances, (3) rush the process, or (4) skip steps in the process. Falling for any of these will prevent us from thriving and will ultimately put us in dangerous places. Avoiding these will enable us to find our strength—God—and grow regardless of the season or circumstance.

BUILD THE WALL IN FRONT OF YOU

The first key to thriving is to focus on building the wall in front of you. Some of the most powerful lessons God wants to teach us are the simplest.

We see this in the strategy Nehemiah laid out for the workers who were rebuilding the walls of Jerusalem. Nehemiah had a powerful encounter with God after hearing a report about the city's fallen walls, and God gave him the assignment to rebuild those walls. When he arrived in Jerusalem, he scouted the walls to determine how bad things really were and what needed to be done. Then he called the priests and the people together to delegate the work.

Nehemiah 3 lists specific individuals or groups to work on the wall and the exact part of the wall they were assigned to rebuild. For the most part, people were assigned to work on the part of the wall that was closest to their homes: "The priests made repairs, each in front of his own house" (verse 28). From what we can gather, Nehemiah said, "Walk out your front door and look directly in front of you. The wall that's directly in front of you—build that."

Simple yet strategic.

This is a powerful picture for how God works in our lives. Sometimes we miss what He is doing right in front of us because ook longingly at other people's portions of the wall, wanting to build those areas. We get distracted watching other people in other assignments and seasons of life, and the grass always looks greener at their section of the wall. We can't see that God is using what is in front of us to develop the root system we so desperately need. The need for significance makes us look at other areas that feel more exciting or more in line with our vision.

We'll never thrive in the process unless we accept the place where God has put us, because that is the only place He will work with us. Faithfulness and obedience call us to recognize what God is asking us to put our hands to and what He is emphasizing in our lives.

I understand why a lot of us have a hard time focusing on what is in front of us, because it usually doesn't look like the promise, dream, or vision we have in our hearts. It takes faith and commitment to trust the God who gave us both the dream and our current assignment and to say, "I don't understand how You're going to get me from here to there. But getting me there is Your job, and this wall in front of me is my job." Faithfulness to build the wall is not giving up your dream; it's trusting God with your dream.

> **Faithfulness to build the wall is not giving up your dream; it's trusting God with your dream.** ✒

I wholeheartedly believe in embracing your dreams and pursuing the passion in your heart. Yet ultimately we are not called to be passionate about a dream but about Jesus and His cause on the earth. Many people I know and respect did not accomplish things for God simply by following their passion but by being faithful and obedient to what God had placed in front of them. This will be tested in your life. Are you more passionate about pursuing a dream or about following Jesus?

As I mentioned in the chapter 1, my first ministry job was as a youth pastor. Jesus Culture was birthed out of the youth group I pastored for over ten years at a church where I was on staff for eighteen years. Even now, as a lead pastor, my heart still leans toward young people and young adults locally and around the world. But it wasn't always like that. When I was twenty-one and my church leaders asked me to be the youth pastor, I turned them down. At the time I did not feel called to young people or the local church. I wanted to travel and preach.

I had read a biography of Billy Graham, and I had also been impacted by some itinerant ministers who had come through our church. That was where I wanted to be building the wall in my life. But eventually I realized God wanted me to build right by my house, and that meant becoming a youth pastor. I said yes to being youth pastor not because I felt a passion for young people but because it was the assignment in front of me.

I'm so glad I accepted that assignment because it set me on a course I am still on today. I had a passion to change the world, but God had to first develop the root system in my life. That root system was developed by putting my hands to the assignment in front of me. I can trace all of the fruit in every area of my life to the eighteen years I spent building the wall in that community.

The problem with making your passion the thing that guides you is that passion can trick you into avoiding tasks that maybe aren't fun but that are absolutely vital to get you to where you need to be. It is important to remember that God can develop your life in different settings. I hear people opt out of opportunities by saying, "I just don't feel a passion for that." While we pursue the vision on our heart, there are a lot of things we are called to do that don't seem terribly exciting but are absolutely vital in getting us to where we need to go.

It's amazing how many believers disqualify themselves and stunt their growth because they don't just do what's in front of them. Do what's in front of you, and do it well. As the Bible says, "Whatever your hand finds to do, do it with your might" (Ecclesiastes 9:10) and "Whatever you do, do all to the glory of God" (1 Corinthians 10:31). If you're delivering pizzas, be the best pizza-delivery person on the planet. If you're answering phones, do it with everything in you. Stay current with the Lord and with whatever assignment He has given you.

> **God is trying to grow you exactly where you are.**

The Enemy is trying to get you off assignment. He wants to distract you with something that God is not emphasizing in your life so that you will miss what God wants to teach you in that moment. Make no mistake: God is trying to grow you exactly where you are.

God is intent on establishing a root system in our life, and we don't always recognize this fact. Because we don't feel passionate about what we are doing, or because it's harder than we thought, or because it's boring or slow, we think we should be somewhere else. But that's not how God works.

LESSON PLANNING

The second key to thriving in God's root-building process is to pay attention to and accept the lessons God is trying to teach you in your current assignment and season. You need to recognize not only what God is asking you to put your hands to but also what He is emphasizing for you and the season in which this is happening.

When I was twenty-five I was asked to lead the second year of the school of ministry at my church, and I did that for four years. To give some context, we began with forty-five students in the second-year class, and when I left, it had grown to over seventy. I knew that wasn't a huge number of students, but I was overwhelmed nonetheless.

Those four years were not fun for me. The students were amazing, but my role was frustrating and exhausting. I was required to do a lot of counseling, put out fires, sit through endless classes, and work through all the administrative needs—none of which I enjoyed and definitely did not feel called to do. I was stretched more than I had ever been stretched before.

For two years I struggled with a feeling that God had given me an assignment that was not a good fit for me. *Why is this so hard?* I wondered. *Is it really supposed to be so hard? What am I supposed to be getting here?* Finally a light bulb turned on. I wondered if the Lord was trying to teach me to love people *through* counseling and pastoring. Was this so hard because I was actually resisting all of this?

That was the answer. It seemed so simple and obvious when I realized it, but it took me a long time to get there. At that point, I said, "All right, Lord. If You're trying to teach me to love people better by sitting with them day in and day out, I'm going to do it."

After that I went into every counseling and pastoring session with a solid commitment to learn to do this. Learning to listen to people's stories and counsel them wasn't easy, but everything about the job became easier once I recognized and embraced the season in which the Lord had me. Beyond counseling, God was teaching me faithfulness in the mundane and the difficult, those things that seemed distant from my vision and didn't fuel me. Would I be obedient to the assignment in front of me even when my passion was not strong?

> **Would I be obedient
> to the assignment
> in front of me even
> when my passion
> was not strong?** ✑

What I didn't see until after that season was over was that those four years were some of the most foundational and critical years for the development of my root system.

The Lord is the teacher. We are the students. He is the One designing our course of study and writing the lesson plans. We thrive in the process when we stop saying "You put me in math—I hate math" and acknowledge "I need to learn math or You wouldn't have put me in here."

In my early ministry life I was blessed to sit weekly under the teaching of Bill Johnson, an incredible teacher. Every week he opened Scripture with such profound revelation and insight, and I was deeply impacted by his teaching. He set the bar high for me as an aspiring preacher. I wanted to be able to receive and teach revelation like Bill and to influence people just as I saw him influencing others.

During this season the Lord began to wake me up around 2:00 or 3:00 in the morning. The first time it happened, I had a strong sense of the Lord's presence. I was confident this was the moment He would drop an amazing revelation on me that would turn into a great sermon.

"Lord, what's on Your heart?" I asked aloud.

I just want to tell you I love you, He said.*

"All right, that's awesome." I paused, waiting for more. "Anything else?"

No, that's it, the Lord said.

The next night I woke up and had the same encounter.

"What is it?" I asked Him. "What do You want to tell me?"

---

* Throughout this book I describe many instances of hearing God personally. I am aware that the phrases "God told me . . ." or "God said . . ." raise questions and concerns for some people. Everything we spiritually sense or hear must be tested by Scripture, which has full authority; however, God tells us that "My sheep hear My voice" (John 10:27) and gives overwhelming evidence that, as His beloved children, we should expect to perceive His communication with us in a variety of ways. Scripture also indicates that it's possible to know the Bible and not know God. For example, Jesus rebuked the Pharisees for searching the Scriptures yet refusing to recognize Him as the One the Scriptures were talking about (see John 5:39–40). Thus we need to know the voice of the Spirit and the Word (Scripture) to understand what God has said and is saying to us presently.

I just want to tell you I love you.

"Okay . . . You told me that last night. Anything else?"

Nope, that's it. I just wanted to tell you I love you.

This happened multiple times—until I finally got it. The Lord had me in a season of learning about His love for me. That was the lesson plan. I had asked for revelation, and that was what He was giving me.

So many people get stuck in their process and don't thrive because they constantly want to be somewhere else, both in what the Lord is teaching them and in what they're putting their hands to. They want the Lord to develop their root systems in the middle of their passions, where they feel most alive. But it doesn't always work like that. We don't get to take only electives when we're building our root system.

Don't Rush

If you are going to thrive in the process, you must not rush it. This is a hard one to get down. It can be very tempting to try to speed up God's time line for building your roots. You must understand that getting out of sync with the timing of God's seasons puts you in danger. Every assignment and lesson He gives you adds something crucial to your foundation. If you don't have all the components of your foundation, then when God adds the weight of your calling and vision to your life, your foundation won't sustain it. The only way to thrive and protect the integrity of what God is building is by saying, "This foundation is going to take as long as it takes to build. Lord, take all the time You need to get me to where You want me to be." And that is harder to do than you think.

Rushing growth is a sign we really don't understand the vision toward which we are growing. We don't understand what God is actually calling us to do. God always calls us to do the impossible.

> **God always calls us to do the impossible.**

He wants to throw us in way over our heads, where He can make us successful according to His definition of success, rather than let us accomplish our own inevitably limited version of the vision. When we see the incredible weight that God wants to put on our lives, we won't want to rush anything in the laying of our foundation. We must recognize that even when things seem to be moving more slowly than we think they should, or even not moving forward at all, the Lord is answering our prayer. He's giving us what we need and preparing us for what He spoke to us.

BURGERS AND GOD'S PROCESS

When I was dating my future wife, SeaJay, I thought I would be romantic and take her on a surprise date. I was working hard to convince her to one day say yes to me. I decided to put together a barbecue picnic and drive her out to a nearby lake. I made hamburger patties, prepared all the toppings, got the drinks together,

borrowed a mini Weber grill, and picked up some charcoal briquettes and lighter fluid.

When everything was ready and hidden in the car, I picked
up SeaJay and drove out to the lake. It was a beautiful evening,
and the lake and the surrounding mountains looked gorgeous in
the setting sun. For some reason (probably because I was twenty),
I hadn't thought too far ahead in my planning. While we were
driving out to the lake, it suddenly hit me: the sun was setting and
it would be dark. I hadn't planned for a date in the dark.

Uh-oh.

I decided the best plan was to give up on the perfect picnic
spot I had in mind and find a place to pull over by the lake. But
mile after mile passed with the lake on one side and a forest on the
other, and I didn't see any place to stop by the lakeside.

I wasn't going to give up, though, so I changed plans again.
Instead of a picnic by the lake, I found a dirt road into the woods
on the other side of the highway and pulled over. And by this
time, it was pitch black outside.

"Um, what are we doing?" SeaJay asked.

"Well, I kind of planned a romantic evening," I admitted.
"We're going to have a barbecue picnic by the lake."

"Right here?"

"Yeah."

"Right *here*?!"

"Yes."

"Banning," SeaJay said firmly, "I'm not getting out of the car."

"What do you mean you're not getting out of the car? I
planned a whole romantic dinner for us!"

"It's dark. We're in a forest. I'm not getting out of the car."

I'm not one to give up easily. Gritting my teeth, I said, "Okay, whatever. Fine. I'll do it myself, then."

When I opened the car door, the dome light came on and I saw SeaJay's face. She was *mad*.

"We're doing this," I pressed. "This is going to be good and romantic, and you'll enjoy this."

Doggedly I pulled out the blanket, laid it on the ground next to her door, and began unpacking the food and setting up the grill.

"You're really not going to get out?" I asked.

"I'm not getting out of this car," she repeated.

"All right."

My next task was to get the grill going and cook the burgers. It happened that I had always used a gas grill and never cooked on briquettes before. How hard can that be? I shook out the briquettes into the grill, doused them with as much lighter fluid as I could, and lit it. Suddenly, I saw exactly where we were. We were right next to a national forest with eight-foot flames shooting up from a grill, and cars were driving by us on the highway.

Nervously, I tried to shield the flames from view. Unaware that I needed to let the coals burn down before I could grill, and feeling increasingly panicked about my furious girlfriend and the idea that I might be arrested for starting a fire by the road, I decided, *I'm just going to throw the burger on the grill now.* I flipped the patties amid the flames and watched as they quickly cooked. A few minutes later, I whipped the burgers off the grill, slid them onto buns with all the toppings I had painstakingly prepared, handed SeaJay a plate through the car window, and sat down on the picnic blanket to eat my burger.

With my first bite, liquid gushed into my mouth. Lighter fluid. My burger tasted like I had marinated it in gasoline.

That was the moment of defeat. I turned to SeaJay and said, "Fine. We don't have to do this. We'll put it all away. Let's go."

I learned something important that night. There are certain things in life you can't rush or manipulate. There's a process to making a good burger, and if you try to rush it, you won't get the results you're looking for. The same is true of God's root-building process in your life.

God feels no pressure to rush or force His plan for our growth. He is calm, steady, and collected even when we want things to speed up. Our frustration will not make God speed up, because He knows we won't get the results we've prayed for.

FEELING BEHIND

Over the years I've realized many people are having a hard time thriving where God has put them because they feel behind. I was thrown off by this in my own life. There was a little voice inside of me always letting me know I was behind. To this day I still have to stem the flood of questions that make me doubt myself and where God has me: "Am I behind? Should I be farther along?"

As a young man in my twenties, my sense of being behind was especially bad. I should know the Bible better. I should be a better preacher. I shouldn't be dealing with some of the struggles

I'm having. I should be a better leader. I should be a better pastor. I should have done this. I should be having a greater impact. *I'm just always behind.*

I read a lot of biographies in those days, and they all reinforced the idea that I was behind. I could tell you that Billy Graham was thirty-one when he met with a US president for the first time, that Martin Luther King Jr. was thirty-five when he won the Nobel Peace Prize. Thomas Jefferson was thirty-three when he wrote the Declaration of Independence. I read those stories and thought, *Billy Graham was thirty-one when he first spoke with a president of the United States? That's only two years away for me! I'm nowhere near any possibility of meeting the president. I'm behind right now. I knew it!*

During this season of feeling behind, I picked up an older minister who was speaking at a conference at our church. On the drive from the church to the hotel, I asked, "What advice would you give young ministers?"

He didn't even blink. "Oh, that's easy," he said. "I'd tell them to stop being in such a hurry to get to the inner place of anointing and to take time to die in the outer court."

Let me explain what he meant by those metaphors. The tabernacle of Moses was the first house of worship in the Bible and served a prophetic role in teaching sinful people how to approach a holy God. In fact, much of the book of Hebrews is dedicated to showing how every aspect of the tabernacle ultimately pointed to and was fulfilled by the ministry of Jesus. The tabernacle was structured with outer and inner courts. The outer court was the place where the priests made sin offerings on a bronze altar; the inner court was the place where the priests, each purified and clothed in priestly garments, offered incense and prayers to God for the people. As New Covenant believers, the outer court symbolizes our call to offer our lives as living sacrifices and renew our minds so we can learn to do the will of God (see Romans 12:1–2). It represents sanctification and character formation—learning to die to the flesh and walk in the Spirit. The inner court represents our priestly ministry—ministering to God through worship and intercession, and ministering to others through teaching and preaching.

The older minister was saying that young ministers have a tendency to rush ahead in ministry and avoid letting God work on their character. They get in a hurry to start impacting people before God has impacted them sufficiently on the inside. Resisting God's root-building process sets them up for difficulties down the road, from ministry burnout to moral failures.

When I heard the minister's words, a huge weight was lifted off of me. *That's what I'm doing,* I thought. *I'm in such a hurry to be out there changing the world that I'm not letting God take His time to shape and prepare me in the way He wants.*

The minister's simple words broke the power of fear and anxiety I had been living under because I felt so behind. *Lord,* I prayed, *I don't want to rush Your preparation in my life. No matter how long it takes, I don't want that feeling of being behind to push me faster than I am supposed to be going.*

It's easy to compare where you are with where you want to be, and to feel a ton of pressure and fear to close the gap in between. But feeling like you're behind and rushing to try to catch up are both off base and harmful. In fact I'll go a step further and tell others, "Don't rush." If you're like me, you need to slow down if you want to thrive in the process. This is counter to our culture, but it is critical if you are going to allow God to develop roots in your life. No one can sprint a marathon. If you want to finish your race, you need to set your pace for the long haul, not a hundred meters.

If you have a garden, you know you can't really do much to speed up plant growth. Gardening is a slow process, and it's easy to get bored and frustrated watering all the plants day after day. It can feel like it's taking forever for anything to grow. But if you try to encourage the plants' growth by watering them twice as long, you'll kill most of them. Plants can only take so much water and nutrients, and can only grow so much in a day. The same is true for us. If we try to rush our growth, we'll only destroy it.

Trust God to get you there in His time. ✍

Trust God to get you there in His time. God will get you to where He wants you, when He wants you there, and how He wants to get you there. If you're not there, it's because He doesn't want you there yet. In our independent, "pull yourself up by your own bootstraps and make it happen" culture, the idea of letting God lead can seem disorienting. But no one can make a God promise happen. The One who promises is the One who fulfills.

Don't Skip Any Steps

Many times we don't even know we are trying to skip steps in God's process because we justify it to ourselves. We think we have a good reason for putting the steps in an order that makes sense to us.

I'm a linear thinker. If you look at my preaching notes, they are laid out in a progressive way: Topic 1, Point 1, Point 2, Point 2A, Point 2A1, Point 2A1a . . . My illustrations are in blue, and Scripture is in red. I need a really good reason to skip any of these steps in my linear planning.

My wife is *not* a linear thinker. Our differences in this area show up all over the place. For example, SeaJay and I have completely opposite approaches when we make macaroni and cheese.

When I make macaroni and cheese, I follow the directions on the box. It says six cups of water, so I use a measuring cup.

If SeaJay sees me, she'll ask, "What are you doing?"

"I'm getting the right amount of water to boil."

"Why?" she'll ask, mystified. "Just fill up the pot."

She doesn't understand that I'm putting six cups of water in the pot because the box says to use six cups of water. Likewise, I'm going to use a measuring cup for the milk and cut the butter exactly where it says on the wrapper to get the right amount of butter. I am going to go through the process step by step, per the instructions on the box.

When SeaJay makes macaroni and cheese, she doesn't use a measuring cup. She fills the pot with water. If I find her doing this,

I'll say, "You don't even know if that's five cups or seven cups! You don't know how many cups are in there!"

Then she'll get the milk and throw some into the pot.

"No! No!" I'll protest. "It's butter first, then the milk. You don't even know how much is in there." In my mind, there is a God-ordained way to make macaroni and cheese, and it is printed on the box.

That's my linear brain at work. But through the years I've discovered something: God thinks a lot more like SeaJay when it comes to building roots in our lives. Root systems do not grow in linear, straight lines. And this drives me crazy. When I'm at A, I think I know exactly what the plan looks like from there on out. I know it's supposed to be A, B, C, D, E, F, and so on. When it turns out to be A, D, V, B, A, I feel justified in protesting and trying to skip or rearrange the steps.

When God spoke to me about my future in my teens and twenties, I immediately started to paint a picture in my head of how it would look, complete with corresponding time lines. At one point, years ago, I was frustrated because some of the plans I had worked out in my head weren't working out in my life.

I sat down with my pastor and told him that the plan wasn't doing what it was supposed to do. And he told me, "It doesn't work like that. What happens is you'll get to the end of your life or you'll get to where you're going, and you'll turn around and say, 'Oh, *that's* how the Lord got me here.'"

I had to learn to surrender my plan and let God order my process.

We're all going to have opportunities to skip or rearrange the steps we see ahead of us. David did. Twice, David ended up right where Saul, his enemy, lay asleep. The Bible says that God put a slumber on the men protecting Saul (see 1 Samuel 26:12). David knew God had ordained him to take over the kingship from Saul, and those moments of Saul's vulnerability looked like obvious divine setups for David to step into his destiny—at least to David's men. "David, kill Saul now," they urged him. "This is the moment that was prophesied. You can be king of Israel right now. All you have to do is kill Saul while he's sleeping here" (see verse 8).

But David refused to skip any steps. He said, "I won't touch the Lord's anointed. If the Lord wants to kill Saul, He can kill Saul. But I won't do it" (see verse 9). David was committed to letting God fulfill His promise according to His plan and time line, and even when opportunities arose, he would not bypass the steps God had laid out for him. David's root system was not yet fully developed. If he had killed Saul prematurely, David's foundation would not have been strong enough for him to be the king God had called him to be.

LEARN TO LOVE THE CAVE

The last key to thriving in the process is to embrace being hidden. The prophet Isaiah describes the hidden work of God as the work of sharpening and honing us into powerful tools and weapons: "He made my mouth like a sharpened sword, in the shadow of his hand he hid me; he made me into a polished arrow and concealed me in his quiver" (49:2, NIV). Being hidden doesn't mean we're isolated from society or withholding our lives from others until we are perfectly polished. But it does mean that we are not seeking a visible platform for whatever we're called to do. It means we are not forcing open any doors that God has not opened. We are waiting for God to put us in front of others at the right time.

For me, one area of being hidden concerned my call to preach. When the church leadership picked somebody other than me to preach, and I thought I was a better preacher than that person, I had to learn to rejoice and say, "God, thank You for hiding my life." You have to learn to love the cave. If you love the spotlight more than the secret place, you're in trouble, because it means you care more about pleasing people than pleasing God. Learn to love when you don't get the credit. Learn to love when you get passed over.

> **Learn to love when you don't get the credit. Learn to love when you get passed over.**

In the cave, you become rooted in faithfulness and obedience to God above all else, and you uproot the weeds of man pleasing and the fear of man.

So take a deep breath and pray, *Lord, thank You for the process in which You have me. You're growing me, teaching me, and wooing me. Thank You for hiding me in the cave and not releasing me too soon. Thank You for protecting me and everyone around me by waiting until I have the right foundation to carry Your promises. Thank You for developing roots in my life and creating in me the strength necessary to sustain what You will release to me. Help me to thrive in the process.*

3

The Trust Factor

The LORD is my rock and my fortress
and my deliverer;
My God, my strength, in whom I will trust.

Psalm 18:2

Every key to thriving in the process requires the same crucial factor: *trust*. Whether it's being faithful to build the wall in front of you, engaging with the lesson of the season, refusing to rush or skip steps, or slowing down and patiently allowing God to get you to where He wants you in His way and on His time line, you'll never do it successfully without trusting Him. Each of these is, in fact, an act of trust. Conversely, any of the things we do to avoid cooperating with God are acts of mistrust. When we fall into coveting someone else's assignment, resisting God's lessons, skipping steps, or trying to promote ourselves, we're actually saying, "I don't really trust You, God."

We must understand that our trust is the main thing God is pursuing as He develops our root system. Trust is what God is building through the process, and trust is what will get us through the process. Trust has two basic elements: *intimacy* and *dependence*. Intimacy and dependence are what Jesus was talking about when He told us to *remain* in Him just as He remained in the Father. He wants us to develop the ability to walk in deep, unbroken intimacy with Him and to depend on Him as He trains and empowers us to become trustworthy partners in His work on earth. The only way He can build this root system of abiding connection is by taking us through a process that asks again and again, "Do you trust Me?" Every time we say, "I trust You," our root system grows. That's how we thrive as He prepares us to bear lasting fruit.

It shouldn't surprise us that the thing God most wants for us is also the thing the Enemy primarily targets and assaults. Every spiritual battle you face—in fact, all of spiritual warfare itself—centers on trust in God. The Enemy uses the same strategy he used in the beginning, when he showed up in the garden:

1. Get God's children to doubt God's trustworthiness.

2. Get God's children to trust something besides God.

The Enemy is dedicated to convincing us that God is either withholding good things or failing to protect us from bad things. He discovers our deepest fears and longings, and he exploits those areas of vulnerability to sow mistrust in our hearts. Every time we experience pain, disappointment, loss, or terror, he tells us that God has abandoned us and that the only thing to do is to protect ourselves. Every time we see some good thing and desire it, he tells us we must take it instead of letting God give it to us in His time and in His way. The Enemy is constantly trying to trick us into mistrusting God, taking matters into our own hands, putting ourselves on the throne of our lives, and ultimately destroying ourselves.

When you look at the history of the Fall and all the destruction that has come from our refusal to trust God, it's difficult to understand why God even trusts us with such a dangerous choice. But the truth remains that He has given us the choice to trust Him, and that tells us it was worth it to Him. He's not intimidated by the Enemy's smear campaign against Him or by our struggle to believe in His goodness when life doesn't feel good. He knows our deepest fears and longings better than anyone, and He is supremely confident that these places of weakness and vulnerability are where He can prove Himself trustworthy to us.

> **We can trust Him with the deep things of our hearts because they are also the deep things of His heart for us.**

That is why God leads us into places of vulnerability where the deep things in our hearts are exposed and where He gets to reveal Himself as our protector and the One who fulfills our deepest desires. He is committed to showing us, through His process in our lives, that we can trust Him with the deep things of our hearts because they are also the deep things of His heart for us.

THE LITTLE TESTS

One of the biggest areas where I have come face to face with this issue is in trusting God with my children, even in the little things that seem trivial and unimportant. For example, when my son, Lake, was eight, he tried out for a local traveling basketball team. Lake loves basketball, and even though I thought he was better than most of the other kids, he didn't make the team.

When I found out he didn't make the team, I was mad. I was mad because I felt so powerless. I did not like that somebody could hurt my son's heart by telling him he was not good enough to play. It felt unjust. For several days I continued to spin over this injustice, telling myself it didn't really matter in the long run, but still not getting over it. Finally, I realized I needed to go to the Lord and figure out why I was having such a hard time. As I prayed through it, I saw what the core issue was.

Lord, I admitted, *I'm not sure if I trust You with my son. I'm not sure I trust You with his heart and his future.*

It seemed silly that something as inconsequential as basketball could reveal my heart to me, but it did. Somewhere in there was a place I was not sure I fully trusted God with my son.

As soon as I saw that place in my heart, I dealt with it. I said, *God, I trust You. I trust You with my kids. I trust You with my son.*

Now, if you had asked me "Do you trust God with your kids?" before this situation, I would have said yes. But then my trust was tested, and though it wasn't a big test, it showed me an area in my heart that had to grow, which gave me an opportunity to let God make it stronger. My roots of trust went down a little deeper.

Incidentally, shortly after I settled that issue with God, Lake made it on to another basketball team that was a much better fit for him. As I sat and watched his games, I often prayed, *Jesus, thank You that Lake got cut from that other team. And thank You for helping me trust You more.*

So many of the trust tests we face in life involve this game of inches over how we respond to the little things that make us feel hurt, disappointed, or scared. The Enemy loves to sow doubt in those little cracks of vulnerability, just like grass seeds find their way into cracks in sidewalks. Over time those seeds can put down roots that chew away at our foundation and compromise our ability to withstand the bigger tests. It's vital we deal with the little tests when they come up. If we can't trust God in the little things, then we aren't going to be able to trust Him in the big things. When God reveals the weak spots in our trust, instead of tolerating them, we can make them stronger by confessing them to the Lord, declaring His trustworthiness, thanking Him for the opportunity to trust Him more, and asking for His grace to do that.

PREPARED FOR THE TESTS

David's journey of building trust started as a boy, caring for his father's sheep. We know he was already a skilled musician and worshiper in this season, because someone recommended him to Saul as a harpist who brought spiritual breakthrough when he played (see 1 Samuel 16:18). David dedicated himself to building intimacy with God through worship. We also know he was learning dependence on God as he fought against lions and bears in the field. When the time came for him to go up against his first big test—Goliath—he was prepared: "The LORD, who delivered me from the paw of the lion and from the paw of the bear, He will deliver me from the hand of this Philistine" (1 Samuel 17:37), he told Saul before he went to face Goliath. That is a declaration of trust.

Jesus Himself was tested in the area of trust by the devil. Jesus didn't stumble blindly into these tests, however; He prepared for them. Alone for forty days in the wilderness, through prayer and fasting, Jesus built intimacy by communing with His Father and built dependence by emptying Himself of His own strength. By the end of those forty days of strengthening His trust in the Father, Jesus was ready for everything the devil threw at Him. His response to Satan's three offers was basically, "I trust God, and I won't mistrust Him by taking matters into My own hands, trusting you instead, or trying to test Him." He beat the devil with trust.

> **Knowing God's name means knowing Him personally and knowing His nature.** 🖋

If you want to build unshakable trust in God and pass your trust tests, you have to let Him teach you intimacy and dependence. These are the roots God is establishing in your life. Inti-

macy and dependence come only through personal knowledge
and encounter. David said, "And those who know Your name will
put their trust in You; for You, LORD, have not forsaken those who
seek You" (Psalm 9:10). Knowing God's name means knowing
Him personally and knowing His nature.

There are plenty of people who use the name of God, and
maybe they know a lot about Him, but it's clear they don't really
know Him, because they don't trust Him and they don't seek
Him. God doesn't expect us to build trust in Him blindly, without knowing His character. He doesn't expect us to build trust
just on what we've heard about Him. He wants us to build trust
on personal knowledge. That's the only way to have true intimacy
and dependence.

LEARNING HIS VOICE

Like David in the field and Jesus in the wilderness, we must allow
God to lead us into a place where we come to know His voice. In
Matthew 4:4, Jesus quoted Deuteronomy 8:3 when He faced the
Enemy in the desert. He told the Enemy the Bible says we don't
just live on bread; we live on every word that "proceeds from the
mouth of God." Not only was that true for Jesus as He wandered
through the desert, it is true for us today. Hearing His voice is
what brings us life. When we don't hear His voice, our hearts and
spirits starve to death. We must set up our lives so we are always
tuning in to His voice. He wants to give us strength and assurance. He wants us to know that He is with us and that we're going
to be okay. His voice is going to get us through the process.

When Lake was about six, he fell off a slide at a playground, landed wrong, and hurt his elbow. At first I thought it was dislocated, so we took him to an urgent-care clinic. They sent us to an emergency room, where an x-ray revealed his elbow was broken. Though the break wasn't severe, the doctor explained, it was in a spot where they needed to insert a pin in order for it to heal properly. Suddenly Lake was facing a night in a hospital and surgery in the morning.

Lake was very nervous when the nurses came to dress him for the surgery. None of my kids had ever been under anesthesia, so this forty-five-minute procedure was a huge deal for him. He was trying his best to be brave, but when the moment came for them to wheel him away from us, clad in a little gown and hat, tears began to roll down his cheeks as he looked back at SeaJay and me.

I walked over to comfort and encourage him, and I made him look into my face as I told him everything was going to be okay. I didn't want him just to hear my words; I wanted him to hear the tone of my voice and see the look in my eyes. If my tone or eyes had contradicted the words coming out of my mouth, I wouldn't have been able to impart much strength and confidence to him. But there was no fear in my voice or my eyes, only steady assurance, and after a few moments Lake calmed down. He continued to gaze at me as they wheeled him away, drawing on the strength I had given him.

This is the kind of connection we need with the Lord, especially as He leads us into moments where we confront our deepest fears and longings. We have to know and be able to stay connected to His voice and His face. In my life, I've realized I'll be okay as long as He's speaking and I'm listening. It doesn't matter what's going on, how many storms I am facing, or how weak and vulnerable I feel. As long as I can quiet my soul before Him and listen when He speaks to me, I'll get through whatever comes. There have been so many times when I have gone to the Lord with some situation that feels overwhelming and heard Him say, *Look at Me. Do I look stressed to you right now? Do I look worried?*

You don't.

Then I don't know why you're worried.

It works every time. If I can hear His voice and see His face, I come back to trust and peace. So I make it my first priority to continually draw close to Him, quiet myself, wait, and listen for His voice.

LEARNING HIS CHARACTER

Along with His voice and His face, we must come to know His character in order to trust Him. The Bible reveals to us that every aspect of God's nature and character proves His trustworthiness and invites our trust, but I'll mention a few that we must discover and hold on to in the process.

First, God cannot lie. When Paul opens his letter to Titus, he introduces himself as "a bondservant of God and an apostle of Jesus Christ . . . in hope of eternal life which God, *who cannot lie,* promised before time began" (1:1–2). Paul was telling Titus, "My credentials are based on promises that are unshakable because they were made by a Father who cannot lie." All God has in Him is truth. He has no ability to lie or mislead. Therefore everything He says and does can be fully trusted.

This aspect of God's nature is hard for us to wrap our heads around, because we have the ability to lie, mislead, and deceive ourselves and others, and we naturally project this onto God. We usually don't admit it, but sometimes we have a picture of God that includes the possibility He could mislead us. We imagine Him placing a dream, a word, a promise in our hearts, then stepping back and telling the angels, "Check this out. They're going to spend quite a few years going after that promise, but it's not going to happen. I just wanted to see them scramble for a while." One of the greatest disciplines of trust is to take such thoughts captive (see 2 Corinthians 10:5) and require our imagination to line up with the truth of His character. The One who promised cannot lie, so no matter how many highs, lows, twists, and turns He takes us through in His process, we can trust that His word is true.

Not only is He a God who cannot lie; He is also a perfect Father. One of the signs that He is a perfect Father, Jesus taught, is that He gives us good gifts:

> If a son asks for bread from any father among you, will he give him a stone? Or if he asks for a fish, will he give him a serpent instead of a fish? Or if he asks for an egg, will he offer him a scorpion? If you then, being evil, know how to give good gifts to your children, how much more will your heavenly Father give the Holy Spirit to those who ask Him! (Luke 11:11–13)

Likewise, James wrote, "Every good gift and every perfect gift is from above, and comes down from the Father of lights, with whom there is no variation or shadow of turning" (1:17). You never have to mistrust anything God gives you, because He only gives good gifts.

God is also loving and kind. Many of us grow up with a picture of God as angry, frustrated, and disappointed in us. We think God must be irritated with us because *we'd* be irritated with us. It's difficult to fathom or accept that He really is as unconditionally loving and kind as He is, especially when we get in touch with our own brokenness and sin. But in the field, where God repeatedly invites us to draw close to Him, our capacity to see and receive His love and kindness begins to grow. And His love and kindness naturally attract and inspire our trust. Psalm 13:5 says, "But I have trusted in Your mercy; my heart shall rejoice in Your salvation."

> **There is nowhere you can go where He is not with you, nothing you can do or say that He does not know.**

Lastly, God is faithful to be *with* us. In Deuteronomy 31:6, when God called Joshua to lead the Israelites out of the wilderness and into the Promised Land, He told Moses to give him this exhortation: "Be strong and of good courage, do not fear nor be afraid of them; for the LORD your God, He is the One who goes with you. He will not leave you nor forsake you."

David also discovered how much God was *with* him, not just physically present, but emotionally present and deeply attuned to the minutest details of David's life:

> O LORD, You have searched me and known me.
> You know my sitting down and my rising up;
> You understand my thought afar off.
> You comprehend my path and my lying down,
> And are acquainted with all my ways.
> For there is not a word on my tongue,
> But behold, O LORD, You know it altogether.
> You have hedged me behind and before,
> And laid Your hand upon me.
> Such knowledge is too wonderful for me;
> It is high, I cannot attain it.
>
> Where can I go from Your Spirit?
> Or where can I flee from Your presence?
> If I ascend into heaven, You are there;
> If I make my bed in hell, behold, You are there.
> If I take the wings of the morning,
> And dwell in the uttermost parts of the sea,
> Even there Your hand shall lead me,
> And Your right hand shall hold me. . . .
>
> When I awake, I am still with You.
>   (Psalm 139:1–10, 18)

The situations God will put you in to build your trust are likely to bring you to a point where you wonder if God is with you at all. Has He abandoned you or forgotten about you? The answer is that there is nowhere you can go where He is not with you, nothing you can do or say that He does not know. He knows you far better than you know yourself, and that is why you can trust Him.

4

Nothing to Prove

I will both lie down in peace, and sleep;
For You alone, O LORD, make me dwell
in safety.

Psalm 4:8

The journey of trust is a two-way street. God not only leads our hearts into greater intimacy and dependence on Him as He builds our root systems, but He also entrusts us with certain assignments, gifts, opportunities, and resources. This other side of the journey of trust is the journey of stewardship, and the goal of stewardship is *faithfulness*. God is looking for partners who will faithfully obey and follow Him as He builds His kingdom on the earth.

If there's anything I've learned about following Jesus, it's that it means living in over your head *all the time*. In my twenties I was certain that the intense feeling of being in over my head would diminish as I got older, but that has yet to happen. God continues to increase the weight of what He asks me to steward and to require growth from my life.

The weight of what God entrusts to us creates pressure in our lives, uncomfortable pressure. As my mentor Bill Johnson told me, "God is not interested in your comfort; He is interested in your growth." One of the reasons He gave us a Comforter is that He knew He was going to be leading us into uncomfortable situations. The question for each of us is not whether we will face uncomfortable pressure in the process but how we should respond to this pressure.

It's important to know there are two different kinds of pressure you will encounter in this growth process. One kind is from God and the other is not. You can recognize them by the direction in which they push you. God is always going to be inviting, nudging, and challenging you to step into greater *faith* and *rest.*

> **God is always going to be inviting, nudging, and challenging you to step into greater *faith* and *rest.*** ✒

The Enemy, however, is going to push you to step into *fear* and *ungodly striving* by trying to make things happen in your timing and through your own wisdom and effort rather than God's. Faith is found in rest, and the Enemy will do anything to get you to buy into his pressure so you will be taken out of rest.

Learning to resist pressure that is not from God is key to faithful stewardship.

SLEEPING IN THE STORM

In Mark 4:35–40 we see one of the best pictures of what it looks like to live from faith and rest, namely, Jesus asleep in the boat during a life-threatening storm:

> On the same day, when evening had come, He said to
> them, "Let us cross over to the other side." Now when they
> had left the multitude, they took Him along in the boat as
> He was. And other little boats were also with Him. And a
> great windstorm arose, and the waves beat into the boat,
> so that it was already filling. But He was in the stern, asleep
> on a pillow. And they awoke Him and said to Him,
> "Teacher, do You not care that we are perishing?"
>
> Then He arose and rebuked the wind, and said to the
> sea, "Peace, be still!" And the wind ceased and there was a
> great calm. But He said to them, "Why are you so fearful?
> How is it that you have no faith?"

We don't get the details about what the disciples were doing before they awoke Jesus, but seeing as He called them "fearful," we can guess that it looked like fear and striving. The seasoned fishermen among them, who had no doubt been caught in many storms, were probably frantically trying to bail out the boat while the others were likely cowering in panic, praying their best desperate prayers to God. Jesus, on the other hand, slept peacefully and then calmed the storm. Both of these are expressions of faith and rest.

As a faithful follower of Jesus, this is what you need to be able to do: sleep in the storm and then calm the storm. You need to be able to rest in the midst of the pressure and then deal with whatever is creating that pressure by standing on the authority God has entrusted to you.

Obviously, there's a learning curve for all of us when it comes to faith and rest, just as there was for the disciples. If we read between the lines, it seems likely that before they got on the boat with Jesus, sleeping in and calming storms didn't exist as options in their minds. You can almost see the "this does not compute" look on their faces when Jesus rebuked them for their lack of faith. Fear and striving were their default reactions in pressure situations, just as they are for most of us. Our learning curve is about unlearning these ingrained responses to pressure and learning new responses based on faith and rest, which God is gracious to teach us.

Faith, the Bible tells us, is "confidence in what we hope for and assurance about what we do not see" (Hebrews 11:1, NIV). So when it comes to this journey of becoming faithful stewards, what is it we must hope for that will give us the confidence to face the storms as Jesus did?

LET THE LORD BUILD THE HOUSE

First, we must put our hope in God's promise to build our house: to fulfill the vision He has put in our hearts to bear lasting fruit, make an impact, and step into the fullness of who He created us to be. Psalm 127:1 says, "Unless the LORD builds the house, they labor in vain who build it." The implication is not that there is no labor involved for us but that we are not to be in the lead position in this building project. God is the architect, the financial backer, the owner, the foreman, the building crew, and pretty much everything else. Our part is to cooperate with God as He builds us and our vision.

There is a rest you enter when you understand *He's* building your house. If you think *you're* building it, you'll end up in fear and striving. The Lord was in my face about this issue early in my ministry. He was constantly telling me to step aside and let Him build my ministry.

The Lord also showed me a principle in Scripture about the nature of ungodly striving and what it produces in our lives. Striving belongs to what the Bible calls the realm of the flesh. The life of the believer is to function solely in the realm of the spirit, not the flesh. John 1:12–13 says, "But as many as received Him, to them He gave the right to become children of God, to those who believe in His name: who were born, not of blood, nor of the will of the flesh, nor of the will of man, but of God." Jesus echoes this two chapters later in His conversation with Nicodemus in which He explained the nature of what it means to be born again: "Flesh gives birth to flesh, but the Spirit gives birth to spirit" (John 3:6, NIV).

Similarly, Paul confronts the church of Galatia about how they have succumbed to the pressure of teachers who insist that in order to be righteous, they must observe the Jewish religious laws in addition to putting their faith in Christ. The apostle tells them they have been trying to add works of the flesh to the work of the Spirit. He gets in their faces about it just as the Lord got in mine: "Are you so foolish? Having begun in the Spirit, are you now being made perfect by the flesh?" (3:3). The Message puts it this way:

> How did your new life begin? Was it by working your heads off to please God? Or was it by responding to God's Message to you? Are you going to continue this craziness? For only crazy people would think they could complete by their own efforts what was begun by God. If you weren't smart enough or strong enough to begin it, how do you suppose you could perfect it? (3:2–3)

There you have it: "Only crazy people would think they could complete by their own efforts what was begun by God." But that's exactly what we do when we give in to the pressure to take over the building of our house, to try to make something happen that only God can make happen.

If God builds the house, He's the One who maintains it. If He opens the door, He will be the One who keeps it open. ✒

I see a lot of people who step into the will of the flesh only to find that fear and striving beget more fear and striving. Flesh gives birth to flesh, which means that instead of relieving the pressure in their lives, they exponentially increase it. Why? Because when they are building the house, they are also responsible for maintaining it. If you open the door, it's your responsibility to keep the door open. But if God builds the house, He's the One who maintains it. If He opens the door, He will be the One who keeps it open.

And those are jobs that only He can do. Many people feel pressure because they are trying to keep open a door God did not open. This is why you must make a sober commitment, saying, *Lord, You'd better open the door, because I'm not opening it. When You open it, I'll step through it.*

WE DIDN'T GET US HERE

When we began releasing albums for Jesus Culture, not many people knew about them. We didn't have a ton of expectations— our own or our audience's—so the pressure around these albums was low. They garnered minimal press, positive or negative.

As things have grown over the years, so has the pressure. Now when we release an album, a lot more people know about it and have opinions about it. The flood of praise and criticism that comes our way can be overwhelming: "This isn't as good as the last one." "Is this it?" "It didn't impact me." "I think they've sold out." "They're all about money now." We experience a lot more pressure about whether people will buy or like our albums than we did with our early work.

But no matter how intense this pressure becomes, I always re-turn to the same place of rest. I simply remember that I don't know how we got here except by following Jesus. Why would I feel pressure to add anything else to stay here than what we did to get us here?

Jesus Culture Band began as the worship team of the youth group I pastored at Bethel Church. Kim Walker, Chris Quilala, and Melissa How led worship during our weekly meetings and youth conferences. We began to encounter God in significant ways during worship, and I thought, *We need to record this. Can we put this on a CD so other people can encounter God like we are?*

We recorded our first CD at one of our conferences. A few people bought it, enough to convince us to try again. As we discussed what should go on the second album, a team member approached me with the idea of recording a DVD with the CD. I asked him how we would do that. He said we just needed to track down some cameras from the people we knew. So we started asking around, "Hey, does anybody have a camera?" One guy said, "I have an XL." Another guy had a GL, and someone else had an old broadcast camera. We brought them together and filmed a DVD for our second album, *We Cry Out.*

People asked us why we did so many cover songs on those early albums. We did it because those songs moved our hearts and led us into encounters with God. We didn't care who wrote them—Phil Wickham, Hillsong United, Chris Tomlin, John Mark McMillan—if we encountered the Lord through a song, we wanted others to experience the same thing.

As we were deciding the set list for *We Cry Out,* Kim suggested a song by John Mark McMillan: "How He Loves." Shortly after we put the CD out with the DVD, we heard that someone had put the video of Kim's singing "How He Loves" on YouTube. We hadn't even thought about putting our stuff on YouTube because it was more for sharing home videos back then, not the worldwide marketing machine it is now.

Sometime later somebody told us that "How He Loves" had 250,000 views. I didn't believe it; that number just blew me away. But it turned out to be the tipping point. "How He Loves" exploded everywhere. We began getting testimonies from around the world. People couldn't stop crying when they watched it. Unsaved friends were seeing the video and giving their lives to Jesus. Pastors were showing it to their congregations as an example of what worship should look like. Leadership conferences were playing it.

We had nothing to do with any of this. We never had a marketing meeting about the album. Even putting it online wasn't our idea. God used someone else to post it. We didn't know what we were doing. It was God who was building the house.

So when pressure wants to creep in to convince us to go into ungodly striving to try to add to what God has done and is doing, we come back to our foundation. We didn't build this, and we don't need to feel any pressure to stay somewhere God brought us to in the first place. We don't need to keep open a door that He opened. If God wants to shut the door, He can shut the door. If He wants to keep it open, He can keep it open. There is so much rest found in that place.

I'm faithful and passionate about doing what God has asked

me to do, but I have no illusions about who is responsible for the growth of Jesus Culture. The moment I start to think I am responsible is the moment I start to step away from my true responsibility.

> **The moment I start to think I am responsible is the moment I start to step away from my true responsibility.**

It's not my responsibility to build or maintain Jesus Culture. It's my responsibility to follow Jesus. Wherever we follow Jesus, that's where I want to be. As long as I rest in the boundaries of that assignment, I am confident I will not give in to the Enemy's pressure to start striving to build the house God is building.

HIS ABILITY TO CHOOSE

The second truth that will enable us to live from faith and rest is that we didn't choose ourselves for this journey of stewardship—God chose us.

In the Bible you'll notice a pattern to the people God chooses. He chooses people who aren't obvious choices, from a human perspective, to do the jobs He wants them to do. David wasn't the obvious choice to be king. Gideon wasn't the obvious choice to fight the Midianites. The disciples weren't the obvious choices to be world-changing leaders. There's a reason God chooses the way

He does. As we saw in David's journey, God chooses those in whom He can develop a strong root system. And it's actually to His advantage to choose those who don't feel qualified for the job, because they are less likely to think they can rely on themselves to make anything happen. Paul pointed this out to the Corinthians:

> Brothers and sisters, think of what you were when you were called. Not many of you were wise by human standards; not many were influential; not many were of noble birth. But God chose the foolish things of the world to shame the wise; God chose the weak things of the world to shame the strong. God chose the lowly things of this world and the despised things—and the things that are not—to nullify the things that are, so that no one may boast before him. (1 Corinthians 1:26–29, NIV)

It's not fun, but it's a good sign you are in the right place when you find yourself praying, *Lord, I feel so inadequate for what You're asking of me and where I am.* This over-your-head journey continually brings you face to face with your insecurities, your weaknesses, and your inadequacies.

In those moments, John 15:16 is my "money" verse. Jesus says, "You did not choose Me, but I chose you and appointed you that you should go and bear fruit." Whenever I feel insecure or inadequate (which is a lot), I pray, *Lord, I do not feel like I have what it takes. I feel so insecure, but I recognize this wasn't~~~~~~ It was Your idea. You chose me, and if You chose me, t~~ have what it takes or You're going to give me what I ne~~*

My confidence is not in my ability to do but in His ability to choose. He didn't choose me so I would fail. He didn't choose me so I wouldn't bear fruit. He chose me so that I'd bear fruit, a lot of fruit, fruit that lasts. That's what I rest in. God chose me, and He didn't make a mistake when He chose me. Sometimes I can't help but wonder why He called me to certain areas when it seems others are better equipped. Nonetheless, God chose me, and I'm not going to second-guess Him, challenge Him, or talk bad about His choice. I'm going to rest in the fact that when I feel inadequate, insecure, and weak, He selected me and this is what He has called me to do.

NOTHING TO PROVE

There's a deeper level of God's choice for us to rest in, and it goes back to John 1:12–13: "But as many as received Him, to them He gave the right to become children of God . . . who were born . . . [by the will] of God." God didn't choose you just to fulfill a particular calling or job for Him; He chose you to be His child.

Before I had children, people told me, "When you have kids, you'll understand the Father heart of God more." I had no grid to understand what they were saying, of course, so I mostly brushed off their words. Then we had our first child. I remember holding her when she was just a month old and gazing, captivated, at her perfect face. I had no idea what her dreams, her desires, or her passions were going to be. I didn't know anything except that I was over-the-top in love with her.

In that moment, I had a revelation: *The greatest thing I'll ever do with my life is raise this child.* Suddenly it seemed that preaching the gospel to stadiums of people around the world could not be as great as raising my daughter. There was nothing I wanted more. A commitment settled in my heart as I looked at her: *I will spend my resources, time, energy, influence—everything I have—to make sure the things in your heart happen.*

As I experienced this intense love for my daughter, another thought came to me. *Is this how God feels about me? He's this committed to doing everything to help me thrive and fulfill my dreams and purpose? If that's true, then what am I worried about?* A huge sense of peace and rest fell over me as I took in this understanding of what it means to have a Dad who is for me.

Several years later I had another encounter with God that drove deeper what it meant to be His son. It happened as I sat in the front row of a Jesus Culture conference morning session, just before I got up to preach.

To give you some background, I had only just begun to preach at our conferences. I facilitated and led the prayer times at these events for about four years before I felt it was time for me to start preaching. Even then, I eased into it by taking the morning meetings. Though I wanted and felt called to preach, I wanted to be sure that the timing was right and that God was asking me to do it.

On this morning, I was not confident in the sermon I was about to preach. On top of this, a powerful meeting had taken place the night before. The meeting had been led by an up-and-coming preacher, a couple of years younger than I, who preached a powerful message that was everything you could want: funny, profound, revelatory, convicting. And then, after the sermon, he had led an incredible time of prayer ministry in which people were touched by the love and power of God in tangible ways.

That morning I sat in the front row with my head in my hands, totally stressed, praying, *God, please don't let my sermon be bad.* I'm sure people thought I was in deep prayer for people in the room to have a fresh encounter with Jesus, but unfortunately I was only praying for myself. I desperately didn't want to look like an idiot in front of the guest speaker who had been so amazing the night before.

Then the Lord spoke to my heart: *Banning, you have a choice. You can either be a preacher or you can be a son. If you decide to be a preacher, you'll be good sometimes and at other times you won't be that good. But if you decide to be a son, you'll be great all the time, because you are a fantastic son.*

Everything changed for me in that moment. I said, *God, I want to be a son. I don't want to be anything else. I don't want to be a preacher. I want to be a son.* From that point on, something shifted for me. I was motivated by something different.

Now, of course, I do want to be a good pastor, a good preacher, and a good leader. But none of that stuff is what drives me, because when I step off a stage and get alone with Jesus, I don't want to hear Him say, *Banning, you're a great preacher.* I want Him to say, *Banning, you're a great son. I love how you love Me. I love how you love people. I love that you're doing the best you can in following Me and being obedient. You're a great son.*

Resting in the truth that God chose you to be His child will shut down the pressure to prove yourself. So many people are driven by the need to prove themselves. "I just want to be really good at [fill in the blank] so others think I've done a good job." But you have nothing to prove. You're not the last kid picked on the playground. God chose you—chose you to be His child and chose you to bear fruit.

> **You're not the last kid picked on the playground. God chose you—chose you to be His child and chose you to bear fruit.** 🖋

You have what it takes because you have Him. He will be faithful to give you all you need so you can be faithful in stewarding what He's entrusted to you. Rest in the fact that God chose you and you have nothing to prove. Let Him build the house while you focus on being a great son or daughter. Let that be what matters most.

5

In over Your Head . . . and Loving It

From the end of the earth
    I will cry to You,
When my heart is overwhelmed;
Lead me to the rock that is
    higher than I.

Psalm 61:2

There's no way around it. God's process of growth in your life is going to involve weakness. This in-over-your-head journey of developing intimacy, dependence, faith, and rest is going to bring you into situations where your natural strength, abilities, and energy are exhausted. It's just part of the deal.

I don't know about you, but I *really* don't like experiencing weakness. I've spent most of my life avoiding weakness. I just don't like being weak at anything.

Some years ago a dear friend of mine and fellow pastor at the church where I was on staff, Eric Johnson, said, "We've put together a running group with some ministry-school students. Do you want to come run with us?"

I hadn't run in about ten years, but I said, "Sure! That'd be fun."

So I got up at 7:00 a.m. and went to meet the group. There were about twenty people waiting when I arrived. Everyone was wearing jogging suits, leggings, and running shoes.

"Wow, you guys are serious," I joked.

Eric smiled. "We're just going to do a three-mile loop."

Not wanting him to know the last time I ran three miles was in high school, I said, "All right, let's go."

Eric was at the front of the group, so of course, that's where I was. In my head I had no doubt I would be in the front for the entire three miles. According to a StrengthsFinder personal assessment, *command* is my top strength, but my second is *competition*. I don't like to lose, especially at sports. I was not going to finish last or at the back of the running group.

The only problem with my plan was that Eric was in great shape, and he set a pace that was a little intense for someone who hadn't run in a decade. Before long, I started to feel like somebody had lit a wildfire in my chest. I thought I was going to have a heart attack and collapse. It was all I could do to hide the fact that I couldn't breathe. Meanwhile, Eric wanted to talk. I tried to just let him talk and every once in a while nod or grunt in agreement.

By sheer force of will, I stayed at the front for the three miles. There was no way I was going to end up in the back. Success! Or so I thought. Unfortunately, the next day it was painful for me to walk. Something was wrong with my Achilles tendon. Days went by and it didn't get any better. Finally, after the problem had bothered me for a month, I went to a specialist.

The specialist examined my ankle for a moment, looked at me, and said, "Let me guess. You're thirty-five."

"How did you know that?" I asked in surprise.

"We see guys like you all the time," he said. "We call you weekend warriors. You think you've still got it. You get out there, and you find out you don't have it."

Somehow I managed to hold back the response I wanted to give him, which was, "Hey, why don't you shut your face and just do your job and make this pain go away!" Instead, I did my best to listen and not react when he told me I had tendinitis and needed to lay off all sports for about six months.

That experience confirmed to me just how much I don't like being weak, how I try to avoid it at all costs, not just in running, but in life. When I read the Bible, however, I not only see that I can't avoid weakness as I follow Jesus, but I also see that I'm supposed to have a particular attitude toward weakness. In the New Testament, everyone from Paul to Peter to James talks about this attitude. They don't talk about tolerating weakness or enduring weakness with gritted teeth. They use words like *joy, rejoice,* and *delight:*

> I *delight* in weaknesses, in insults, in hardships, in
> persecutions, in difficulties. (2 Corinthians 12:10, NIV)

In this you greatly *rejoice,* though now for a little while, if
need be, you have been grieved by various trials. (1 Peter 1:6)

Consider it pure *joy,* my brothers and sisters, whenever
you face trials of many kinds, because you know that the
testing of your faith produces perseverance. Let perseverance finish its work so that you may be mature and
complete, not lacking anything. (James 1:2–4, NIV)

Not only that, but we *rejoice* in our sufferings, knowing
that suffering produces endurance, and endurance produces character, and character produces hope, and hope
does not put us to shame, because God's love has been
poured into our hearts through the Holy Spirit who has
been given to us. (Romans 5:3–5, ESV)

This attitude is completely upside-down and counter to my
natural attitude toward weakness, and I don't think I'm the only
one. Hardship, suffering, trials, persecution—these are not experiences we naturally associate with joy. Any experience that attacks
our strength triggers fear and insecurity, which is usually the opposite of *delightful,* so the idea of trying to enjoy weakness strikes
most of us as weird, almost wrong. Where do Paul, Peter, and
James come up with this attitude of rejoicing in weakness?

They all give the same reason. Experiencing weakness gives us
access to two things we can get in no other way: proven faith and
supernatural strength.

The God Who Raises the Dead

One of the most popular verses on faith is Hebrews 11:6: "Without faith it is impossible to please God" (NIV). I've heard many sermons quote that verse. We applaud it. We highlight it in our Bibles. We hang up posters of that verse. We love the concept of faith and pleasing God with faith; we just don't like being put into positions where faith is required. Faith is proven at the point of our weakness and emptiness, the point where all is lost if God doesn't show up. That's a place we avoid and don't naturally love to be.

Probably one of the weakest, most desperate moments during David's years of preparation for the throne came when they were almost over, just before he was crowned king. David and his men returned from battle to find their city, Ziklag, burned to the ground and all their wives and children gone, abducted by the Amalekites. Utterly devastated, "David and the people who were with him lifted up their voices and wept, until they had no more power to weep" (1 Samuel 30:4). After spending himself in grief, David then had to deal with the sudden anger and threats of his people: "Now David was greatly distressed, for the people spoke of stoning him, because the soul of all the people was grieved, every man for his sons and his daughters" (verse 6). Between this doubled grief and distress, David had absolutely nothing left. He had only two options: allow the people to kill him or see if God would show up. After "David strengthened himself in the LORD his God" (verse 6), he asked the Lord to give him a word about what to do.

The Lord told him, "Pursue, for you shall surely overtake them and without fail recover all" (verse 8).

In total weakness, David put his faith in the God of the impossible, and he not only avoided being killed but ended up receiving strength to completely restore the situation that had almost taken him out.

This wasn't the only time David encountered weakness in his life, nor is David the only one in Scripture who experienced God's showing up at their moments of weakness. Scripture gives us story after story of how God led people through impossible situations, but we often read these stories like fairy tales and forget they really happened. There was actually a guy named Jonathan who walked three miles with his armor bearer and took on the Philistine army. There was a guy named Daniel who was thrown into a den of real lions, and his friends were thrown into a real fiery furnace. If God hadn't shown up, it wouldn't have worked out for these guys. This is the same God who calls us to a Christian life that is impossible unless He shows up.

In his letters, Paul described desperate, life-threatening situations *all the time.* In 2 Corinthians, he wrote,

> We do not want you to be uninformed, brothers and
> sisters, about the troubles we experienced in the province
> of Asia. We were under great pressure, far beyond our
> ability to endure, so that we despaired of life itself.
> Indeed, we felt we had received the sentence of death.
> But this happened that we might not rely on ourselves
> but on God, who raises the dead. (1:8–9, NIV)

"Far beyond our ability"—that's weakness. "The sentence of death" goes even deeper—you can't get much more to the end of yourself than the moment you think you're about to die. But in those moments, they discovered who was with them—the God who raises the dead. They found that when they came to the end of themselves, there was One they could rely on, and they put their faith in Him.

This is exactly what Abraham, the father of faith, built his faith upon: the God who raises the dead. His two great acts of faith—believing God's promise to give him a son and then offering up that son at God's command—were both based in his belief that God could raise the dead:

> [Abraham] is our father in the sight of God, in whom he believed—*the God who gives life to the dead* and calls into being things that were not. . . .
>
> Without weakening in his faith, he faced the fact that *his body was as good as dead*—since he was about a hundred years old—and that *Sarah's womb was also dead.* (Romans 4:17, 19, NIV)
>
> By faith Abraham, when God tested him, offered Isaac as a sacrifice. . . . *Abraham reasoned that God could even raise the dead,* and so in a manner of speaking he did receive Isaac back from death. (Hebrews 11:17, 19, NIV)

It's one thing to say we believe God raised Jesus from the dead and that we have the hope of eternal life through faith in Him. It's another thing to put our faith in the God who raises the dead as He leads us into experiences of weakness. This is where our faith gets real. But when you discover that He is the One always with you, the One you can rely upon, it changes everything.

In the Deep End

In my life the greatest pressure I've experienced occurred in the years when we started doing Jesus Culture conferences in large stadiums. Our first big stadium event was at the Allstate Arena in Chicago in 2011. The Lord led us to plan this event four years before it took place, and He gave us clear guidance for each step of the journey to get there. It was exciting to pray and wait for Him to speak, but there was also a ton of pressure as we took each step in faith. We were so encouraged when fourteen thousand people showed up for the event. It was an overwhelming success in every aspect.

After that monumental gathering, I sensed the Lord saying, *That was just the beginning. I want you to keep moving forward.*

In response, I prayed and asked God to clearly reveal the steps ahead in the same way He had over the four years leading up to Chicago. But the Lord impressed on me that He would not be leading me in the same way as we moved forward. He wasn't going to be as loud and obvious as before, because He was requiring a different level of faith from me and my team.

We decided to do two gatherings in 2012, one in Los Angeles and one in New York City. We booked the Nassau Veterans Memorial Coliseum on Long Island, which seats thirteen thousand,

and the Nokia Theater in Los Angeles (now the Microsoft Theater), which seats seven thousand and hosts events like the *American Idol* finale and the American Music Awards.

The year leading up to those events made the four years before Chicago seem like a vacation. I had never experienced such overwhelming pressure, never wrestled so intensely, never experienced weakness at that level. The financial risk we took kept me awake at night. The numbers weren't there. The stress was causing major conflicts in relationships. It was crazy. Yet somehow I held on to the Lord's word that He was requiring more faith from me. Being out "far beyond my ability" was terrifying, but it also meant I was not playing it safe. I didn't want to get to the end of my life and say, "I never really did anything that required faith. I only did things if the finances were there, the people were there, and success was guaranteed. I never really did anything that required me to trust God." That thought was the one thing that kept me going.

We did the conference in New York City first, and it was amazing. God was faithful, as He always is, to meet with people in a significant way. We had powerful times of worship, and one of my favorite worship albums was recorded there. But only five thousand people came to an arena with a capacity for thirteen thousand. The entire top level of the Nassau Coliseum was empty, and the bottom level was only partly full.

On the first night I looked out at the crowd, accepting the fact that we were looking at a big financial hit. Then I sensed the Lord's voice as I had at the beginning of this journey.

I wanted you here, He said. *I needed you to experience this.*

From the outside, this sounds a lot like a certain picture of

God many people have in their minds. They think God is like a dad who thinks the best way to teach his kid to swim is to throw her into the deep end of the pool and walk away. I mean, why else would God ask me to step out in faith only to let me end up way over my head? Did He just toss me in the deep end and leave me to figure it out?

No. That's not how God works. Yes, He invited me into the deep end, but He didn't walk away. He was right there, in the deep end, with me. That's what He needed me to experience. He needed me to know that He was with me in weakness. In a moment that felt in many ways like a failure, a death, a loss, He was there saying, *This story is not over. I'm the God who raises the dead. I've got this covered and I've got you covered.* God had drawn close to me at one of the most vulnerable moments in my life. He again showed His faithfulness to us financially and in every way.

There is an intimacy with God we can only experience in moments of weakness. There are things about Him we can only get to know in those times. This is the theme of Psalm 23:

> Even though I walk through the valley
>   of the shadow of death,
>   I will fear no evil,
> for you are with me;
>   your rod and your staff,
>   they comfort me.
>
> You prepare a table before me
>   in the presence of my enemies;

you anoint my head with oil;

   my cup overflows. (verses 4–5, ESV)

David didn't say, "You get rid of all of my enemies." He said, "Right here, with death hanging over me and with enemies surrounding me, You are with me. You're communing with me, feeding me, and creating intimacy with me in this place of weakness and dependence."

When we come through that valley of the shadow of death, when we emerge out of the deep end, then what? We have an awareness of God's abiding presence that forever changes the way we see impossible situations. Knowing that He is with us even in the deep end diminishes the pressure and anxiety around our taking risks. Put simply, we have a deeper, stronger faith. Our roots are firmly established in the revelation of a Father who never leaves us.

> ## Nothing is worth more to God than our faith.

Nothing is worth more to God than our faith. It's what pleases Him, and He loves to put us in situations where we can please Him. He also loves to put us in situations where *we* get to experience and see that our faith is genuine. Consider the following passage:

> In this you greatly rejoice, though now for a little while, if need be, you have been grieved by various trials, that the genuineness of your faith, being much more precious than

gold that perishes, though it is tested by fire, may be found
to praise, honor, and glory at the revelation of Jesus Christ.
(1 Peter 1:6–7)

In those moments when we feel like we don't have anything
more, God says, *You're in a great situation! You're in the fire, but
it means that you're about to find out that your faith is genuine.
You can't find that out when everything is going great for you. You
can only find that out in the fire. And that's more important than
any gold that perishes, any money you could ever get.*

Tested, proven, genuine faith comes when we let God lead us
into weakness. That is a reason to rejoice.

SUPERNATURAL STRENGTH

God doesn't call us to just endure weakness; He tells us that we
should also rejoice in our weakness. Paul said that weakness is the
door to a strength that is far greater than our own: Christ's. Jesus
Himself told Paul, "My power is made perfect in weakness." Paul
obviously thought Christ's perfect strength was a prize worth suffering weakness for, because he added, "Therefore I will boast all
the more gladly about my weaknesses, so that Christ's power may
rest on me. . . . For when I am weak, then I am strong" (2 Corinthians 12:9–10, NIV).

In chapter 1, I said that the people who most impress me are
not those who start strong in their race in God but those who finish the race strong, especially because the race is a marathon, not
a sprint. Along with physical stamina, there's a different kind of

focus, a certain emotional and mental energy needed to run the long race, and that's the kind of strength Christ perfects through our weakness. It's the strength to get up after each stumble, the strength to keep moving forward, the strength to fight another day. The Bible says, "Do not lurk like a thief near the house of the righteous, do not plunder their dwelling place; for though the righteous fall seven times, they rise again, but the wicked stumble when calamity strikes" (Proverbs 24:15–16, NIV). When Christ, our righteousness, perfects His strength in us, we may get knocked down, but we never stay down.

> **If we do not let God perfect His strength in our weakness, we won't be able to endure and finish the race.** ✎

If we do not let God perfect His strength in our weakness, we won't be able to endure and finish the race. Consider the parable of the sower. When Jesus explained this parable to His disciples, He said that the seed is the Word and the soil represents different kinds of people. The stony soil represents those who, "when they hear the word, immediately receive it with gladness; and they have no root in themselves, and so endure only for a time. Afterward, when tribulation or persecution arises for the word's sake, immediately they stumble" (Mark 4:16–17).

Stony soil is a perfect metaphor for people who have never learned to embrace weakness and vulnerability. Their reliance on their own strength creates a hardness, a resistance to God's building a root system in their lives. Thus the first time God leads them into inevitable hardships and persecutions, they have no endurance. They stumble and don't get up. That's not where we want to be.

DAILY BREAD

It seems counterintuitive, but one of the ways we embrace weakness and receive Christ's strength to endure for the long journey is to do what Jesus taught in the Sermon on the Mount: "Do not worry about tomorrow" but pray "Give us this day our daily bread" (Matthew 6:34; 6:11). Christ's strength can only come to us in the present moment to meet a present need. As you experience His faithfulness to give you His strength continually, day by day, you become free to run after the things He has called you to do and embrace them as an adventure.

I was at a conference with some friends from the Crow Nation in Billings, Montana. I was so impacted by their hunger for revival, not just for the Crow Nation or the people of the First Nations, but also for revival in America. My heart was immediately knit to this incredible community of people. I also fell in love with the stunning land of their reservation. Some of the most beautiful countryside in the world is in Montana. When I told them I would love to see more of their land, they said, "Anytime you want to come, come. We have a place for you. Come, enjoy the land."

This was enticing, but I'm not a big camper, fisherman, or hunter. My brother-in-law, however, is. So when I got back home, I asked him if he wanted to visit the reservation with me. He jumped at the opportunity, and so I began to plan a trip. My first task was to find the right gear. The only thing I knew I had was an old pair of boots my brother-in-law had given me ten years earlier, so I hunted around the house until I found them. Then I started asking friends if they had anything I could borrow. A friend gave me his high-tech, low-temp mummy sleeping bag and a camp stove. After scrounging a few more items, I decided I would have to buy some appropriate clothing. As I stepped into an REI store for the first time in my life, I couldn't help feeling like the employee was judging my skinny jeans as she helped me find some camping apparel and the other things I needed. Soon after, my brother-in-law and I headed to Montana.

The land was as spectacular as I remembered it. My friends took us out in their four-by-four to a river bend, put up a tent, and left us to enjoy the wilderness. That first night was fairly cold in my city-boy estimation, but I survived. The next night, my friends came back and helped us put up a tepee so we could experience a night in one. Unfortunately, the tepee was less insulated than the tent had been, and I was even colder that night. I wore all my clothes inside the mummy bag and was still *freezing*. So the next night I booked a hotel room and had one of the best nights of sleep of my life.

I hate to admit this, but if you put me alone in the middle of the wilderness, my chances of survival would be slim. Many of us imagine this is how God operates in our lives. He drops us unprepared into the wilderness—which is terrifying and ultimately fatal for us—and tells us to figure it out on our own. But God doesn't really dump us in the wilderness and leave us to figure it out. He comes with us, and He comes fully equipped for the journey. Because He is with us, the place where we would have died on our own becomes a place where we can actually thrive and find joy. Whenever we feel alone on this journey, whenever we feel weak and inadequate, whenever we feel unprepared for what is ahead, it's in those places we encounter God at a new depth. We can rejoice in our weakness because it gives God—who has way more stuff than REI—a chance to show off all His cool stuff and make life exhilarating.

EMBRACE WEAKNESS

As I look back at all the times God has displayed His strength in my life over the years, every time, unsurprisingly, was a moment when I felt weak and inadequate. But as I put these moments together, I realized I had never made the choice to embrace my weakness as a necessary part of His showing up in my life.

Since that realization, I have been on a journey to embrace my weakness. I want to get to the place where, like Paul, Peter, and James, I truly rejoice and delight in weakness, trials, persecution, and suffering, because I know that God is going to show up, prove my faith genuine, and prove Himself strong.

Jesus Himself embraced weakness. He became totally broken, empty, and spent, to the point of death. And then the God who raises the dead showed up. History changed when God perfected His strength in Christ's weakness, and I believe we will change history as we invite Christ to do the same in ours.

6

Beyond the Feelings

The law of the LORD is perfect, converting
    the soul;
The testimony of the LORD is sure, making
    wise the simple;
The statutes of the LORD are right, rejoicing
    the heart;
The commandment of the LORD is pure,
    enlightening the eyes. . . .
Moreover by them Your servant is warned,
And in keeping them there is great reward.

Psalm 19:7–8, 11

SeaJay's granny is ninety-three years old and lives on the same farm in Vacaville, California, where she grew up. The first time I visited the farm, I noticed a huge orange tree standing on the lawn, laden with ripe fruit. This was a novelty for me, having grown up in the suburbs where we didn't have big fruit trees in our yards, so I walked over to admire the tree. When I asked Granny if I could have an orange, she told me I could have as many as I wanted.

I picked an orange and peeled it, inhaling its fresh citrus aroma. When I popped the first wedge in my mouth, I thought I must be eating the most delicious orange I had ever had in my life. It was the most perfect, melt-in-your-mouth experience of ripeness, juiciness, and sweetness. I immediately took her up on her offer and had more. From that moment, the orange tree became one of the things I looked forward to whenever we visited Vacaville. I would always remember, *I'm going to get an orange!*

I asked Granny why the oranges were so unbelievably good. She explained that the soil in Vacaville is particularly deep, rich, and loose, and tree roots are able to go deep and thrive in it. Good roots in good soil create good fruit.

In order to develop a thriving root system, our lives must be rooted in the soil of Scripture. There are many areas where God develops your root system, but none is more important than going deep in the Word of God. David understood this, and he likened those who meditate on the law of the Lord (Scripture) to a fruitful tree planted by water:

> But his delight is in the law of the LORD,
>   And in His law he meditates day and night.
> He shall be like a tree
>   Planted by the rivers of water,
>   That brings forth its fruit in its season,

Whose leaf also shall not wither;
And whatever he does shall prosper. (Psalm 1:2–3)

Delighting and meditating obviously go beyond mere reading. If we want a firmly planted root system founded on the Word, we must go deep in the Bible—chewing on it, studying it, memorizing it, praying it, and especially *doing* it.

David delighted in and meditated on the Word of God. Though many of the psalms reveal his deep knowledge of the books of Moses (the Scriptures of his day), perhaps none does more than Psalm 119, the longest of all the psalms. This 176-verse poem is entirely dedicated to describing David's value for the Torah, the law of God, and all the ways it informed, strengthened, protected, and led his life. His foundation was built on Scripture.

As we have seen thus far, the root system God wants to build in our lives is a root system of complete trust in, dependence on, intimacy with, and faith in Him. This is why He leads us into both trust tests and deep-end experiences. But God doesn't expect us to know and trust Him solely through these personal experiences; He is also revealed through the established, authoritative record of how He has revealed Himself to millions of people throughout history, namely, the Scriptures. He wants the *truth* about who He is as revealed in the Scriptures to lead us into *faith* and *trust*. The apostle Paul wrote, "So then faith comes by hearing, and hearing by the word of God" (Romans 10:17). It's when your roots go deep in the soil of the Word that you develop an ability to hear Him, and when you can hear Him, faith comes.

Mandate to Follow

The mandate for every Christian is first and foremost to follow Jesus. But we won't know where to follow Jesus unless we see where He is going, and the first place to discover where Jesus is going is found in the Bible. The Bible reveals Jesus and holds His teachings, upon which our lives are to be founded.

Jesus wants us to know Him through the Scriptures. He *expects* us to know Him through the Scriptures. If we want His word to abide in us, Jesus said, then we need to come to Him through the Scriptures. He rebuked the Pharisees for not doing this:

> But you do not have His word abiding in you, because whom He sent, Him you do not believe. You search the Scriptures, for in them you think you have eternal life; and these are they which testify of Me. But you are not willing to come to Me that you may have life. (John 5:38–40)

The sign that His word abides in us is that we search the Scriptures, and they lead us to faith and eternal life in Jesus.

After Jesus was crucified and buried, two of his disciples were walking on a road and feeling discouraged and confused. They had believed that this man they had followed for three years was the Son of God, the Messiah, and that He would save the nation of Israel. Instead, He had died in disgrace, and their faith and hope were shattered.

Then the resurrected Jesus, whom they did not recognize, began to walk alongside them on the road. He asked them why they were so sad, so they told Him about the devastating loss of their hero. They even mentioned that they had heard the report of women at the tomb who claimed that Jesus was alive, but they said they were skeptical since none of the disciples had seen Him.

Jesus could easily have said, "Those ladies were right! I'm alive!" Instead, He scolded them for their unbelief and began opening up the Scriptures to them: "And beginning at Moses and all the Prophets, He expounded to them in all the Scriptures the things concerning Himself" (Luke 24:27). He wanted their recognition of Him to be based in the Scriptures. Not until just before He vanished from their sight did He open their eyes so they could recognize who He was. But by that point, it wasn't seeing Him that convinced them. "Did not our heart burn within us while He talked with us on the road, and while He opened the Scriptures to us?" (verse 32) they asked. They knew Him because He had revealed Himself through the Scriptures.

> **They knew Him because He had revealed Himself through the Scriptures.**

As many of His teachings in the Gospels reveal, Jesus Himself was immersed in and rooted in the truth of Scripture, which is perhaps the greatest reason for us to be immersed and rooted in Scripture as well. If Jesus studied, spoke, believed, and practiced the Scriptures, then all who follow Him must do the same. One of the most powerful ways Jesus used the Scriptures was during His temptation. When Satan tested Jesus in the wilderness, Jesus's default response was "It is written" (Luke 4:4, 8) and "It has been said" (verse 12). The devil's lies and peer pressure could not manipulate Him because He had dedicated Himself to knowing and doing the Word of God.

BUILT ON THE ROCK

Jesus's foundation must be our foundation. Jesus concluded His mind-blowing Sermon on the Mount with the following statement: "Therefore whoever hears these sayings of Mine, and does them, I will liken him to a wise man who built his house on the rock: and the rain descended, the floods came, and the winds blew and beat on that house; and it did not fall, for it was founded on the rock" (Matthew 7:24–25).

> **Every aspect of my experience needs to be tested and understood through the lens of Scripture.** ✍

One of my concerns about the church right now is that our lives are being built on the shifting sands of our feelings rather than on the rock of doing the sayings of Jesus. We live in a society that is guided by what *feels* right, and this has slipped into the church. You hear people say, "That just doesn't *feel* like God." But neither feelings nor popular opinion, which so easily sways our feelings, determine truth in our lives or society. Truth is not rooted in our feelings or opinions, but in Scripture.

My intent is not to diminish the value of our emotions. I value emotion and connect to God emotionally, along with other dimensions of my being. And I believe that when the Lord speaks to me, there is an emotional component to that experience. However, every aspect of my experience needs to be tested and understood through the lens of Scripture.

A few years ago, a book that came out was theologically controversial. I followed the controversy a bit and came across a video blog of someone defending the message of the book. He told a story about a man who got a puppy and poked the puppy's eyes out. The blogger argued that since he couldn't imagine a good person doing something so cruel, he couldn't imagine that a good God would do cruel things, like sending people to hell. That was his defense of the message of the book.

I remember watching that video and thinking, *I don't want to know what you think God would or wouldn't do. I want to know what Scripture says.* What we imagine God to be like shouldn't come into the conversation. The Bible has to come before our feelings or imagination. The default question when looking at any area in our lives or society must be, "What does the Bible say about this?"

I learned to ask this question in my late teens. I grew up in a very conservative environment that was actively opposed to the working of the Holy Spirit. In fact, they viewed people who claimed to practice the gifts of the Spirit as under demonic influence. I didn't question these beliefs until I was seventeen. I encountered the Lord in a deep way and developed an insatiable hunger for the Bible. I decided to read the Bible through in twelve months but ended up reading it in ten months because I couldn't put it down. I was determined to find out what the Bible said about the gifts of the Spirit. I had no commentaries, but I had a Ryrie study Bible, which had lists of cross references in the margins. I would find a verse about a subject, read it, and then read all of the cross-referenced verses for that verse. I began to solidify and strengthen what I believed based on what I read in Scripture, which diverged significantly from what I had been taught when I was growing up.

The Bible has to come before our feelings or imagination. ✍

Since then I have been passionately committed to testing everything I am taught by the truth of the Scriptures. In my experience, however, many Christians seem to have lost the priority of testing everything by the Scriptures. We have come to believe that what we feel is truth, and we are not continually going back to Scripture to find truth. If you are going to navigate this root-growing process well, it is critical you know the truth of the Word.

This journey in which God is developing your roots will put you in uncomfortable positions. It's common for people to enter environments where God is moving and to feel uncomfortable. Many reason, *I just don't think Jesus would make me feel uncomfortable, so this must not be God.* Your comfort level should not be the thing that determines whether you can believe something is of God or not. When you read the Bible, you will find many accounts of God's showing up that involved making someone uncomfortable. Take the disciples on a stormy night on the Sea of Galilee, for example. They suddenly saw a glowing figure walking toward them on the water: "They were troubled, saying, 'It is a ghost!' And they cried out for fear" (Matthew 14:26). The disciples' comfort in that moment didn't determine whether or not Jesus was walking toward them. He did not have a problem with making them feel uncomfortable.

Life is going to be full of moments of discomfort and uncertainty. Jesus Himself told us that rains, floods, and winds would assault our houses. The only way we will withstand such pressures is by having our foundations solidly built, our roots firmly planted, in knowing and doing the Scriptures. That is the only rock we can stand on in the swirl of conflicting emotions and perceptions.

SCRIPTURE TELLS US WHO WE ARE

Being rooted in the Scriptures will not only help us stand on the firm foundation of truth instead of on our thoughts and emotions, but it will bring correction and order to our internal world so our thoughts and emotions will come to reflect the truth. Ultimately, we must learn to bring every aspect of who we are, from our beliefs to our personalities, temperaments, and behavior styles, under the authority of Scripture.

I was invited to teach at a school of ministry in Atlanta, and I decided to talk to them about the issue of community. I spent a couple of hours talking through what the Bible says about community and the examples in Scripture in which we see how people lived that out. I emphasized how much we needed to be doing life with people and how vital it was for us not to be isolated. At the end of the session I took some questions, and a woman raised her hand.

"I actually really like being by myself," she said. "I think it's okay to be alone." She wasn't being defiant, just honest.

I understood what she was saying, because I am an introvert. I love being by myself and get recharged when I am alone. I believe God loves introverts and extroverts alike and that He created us with these facets of our personalities. However, even these natural inclinations in us must come under the authority of Scripture. As an introvert, I know that it can be tempting to think that I can live a full Christian life on my own, with just me and Jesus. On the other hand, I know extroverts who lean toward depending on a group for their spiritual life. The Bible brings correction to both bents by teaching that we are to live out our faith in community and develop accountable relationships, but also that we should get alone with God on a regular basis and develop a rich devotional life. Scripture doesn't shut down our bents or temperaments; it shows us how they can be expressed in healthy ways.

After explaining this, I said to the woman, "I've tried to open up Scripture to you. You don't have to believe anything I say, but if you want to grow in God, you do need to know what the Bible says about God's design and order for your life. Build your thoughts on what the Scriptures say and on nothing else."

The truth of the Scriptures will also bring health and order to our emotions. Our emotions are very much connected to whatever we are meditating on and believing. If we want to be able to trust that our emotions are reflecting the truth, then we must hold them up to the truth of the Scriptures. How common is it for people to experience powerful emotions connected to negative beliefs about themselves or God? "I feel like God is angry with me. I feel like God is disappointed. I feel like God is mad. He's not going to take care of me. There is no hope." All of these are lies, no matter how real they feel. If you want to align your emotions with truth, you need to go to the Word and find out what God says and thinks about you.

> **Build your thoughts on what the Scriptures say and on nothing else.**

Do you know how to determine the value of something? Find out the highest price people are willing to pay for it. If I want to find out what my wedding ring is worth, I could ask people, "How much are you willing to pay for this?" The highest bidder will tell me what it's worth. Likewise, when struggling to know our value, we must look at the Scriptures and see what God was willing to pay for us. The price He paid was so huge that we can't fathom it. He paid the price of becoming one of us, of serving us, of suffering for us, of dying for us, of raising us up with Him.

The testimony of the value in which He holds each of us and of what He thinks of us in the Scriptures is overwhelming. If you want a good place to start reading about it, go to Romans 8:

> There is therefore now no condemnation to those who are in Christ Jesus. . . .

And we know that all things work together for good
to those who love God, to those who are the called
according to His purpose. . . .

If God is for us, who can be against us? He who
did not spare His own Son, but delivered Him up for
us all, how shall He not with Him also freely give us
all things? . . . Yet in all these things we are more than
conquerors through Him who loved us. For I am per-
suaded that neither death nor life, nor angels nor princi-
palities nor powers, nor things present nor things to come,
nor height nor depth, nor any other created thing, shall be
able to separate us from the love of God which is in Christ
Jesus our Lord. (verses 1, 28, 31–32, 37–39)

That's just part of one chapter in this amazing book, and if
that doesn't make you *feel* some things, you're not reading it right.
Delight and meditate on that *until* you start to feel it. That's when
you know your roots are getting planted in the Word.

PEER PRESSURE

When we were in Chicago a few years ago, I fulfilled a dream of
seeing a baseball game at Wrigley Field. It was a fantastic experience that definitely lived up to my expectations. But during the
game I witnessed one of the most intense peer-pressure situations
I have ever seen.

There's a tradition at Wrigley that when the opposing team

hits a home run, whoever catches the ball throws it back on the field as a sign of defiance. I can't remember in which inning it was, but one of the visiting players homered into the left-field stands. The eyes of forty thousand fans all turned in that direction. I couldn't see what was happening from my seat in the upper deck, but apparently someone picked it up, because the crowd started chanting, "Throw it back! Throw it back! Throw it back!" Seconds ticked by, but the person with the ball wasn't throwing it back. The chanting went on for a bit longer, and then suddenly, it changed to a chorus of boos. I've never heard anything like it before—those boos were deafening. The poor fan held out for about fifteen seconds. Then, just as the tension reached its peak, everyone saw a baseball go *boop!* out onto the field, and the place went ballistic. Forty thousand people cheered like mad, because they got that fan to throw a ball back.

Our society comes at us very hard in all areas of belief systems. There is a lot of peer pressure to convince us what truth is, and it is all based on feelings: "Well, that just doesn't feel right, does it? I can't imagine a God who would do that."

If we don't have our roots in Scripture, we are going to be in serious trouble when peer pressure comes against us to tell us what "truth" is. Before we know it, we're going to wake up and realize that at some point we stopped following Jesus and started following the voice of the crowd. If we are not only to resist the peer pressure of our culture but are also to push back with the pressure and influence of the kingdom—which is our mandate—then we must put our roots down deep in the Word.

MANDATE TO LEAD

Our mandate to follow Christ is also a mandate to lead. As we follow Christ, we are to make a way for others to follow us, just as the apostle Paul said: "Follow my example, as I follow the example of Christ" (1 Corinthians 11:1, NIV). We are leaders because we are followers. Though each of us will lead different people in different arenas and different ways, we must embrace the fact that following Jesus makes us leaders.

Taking responsibility as a leader means accepting that your life affects others and that you will always produce others who are like you. The influence of dysfunctional, broken leaders produces dysfunctional, broken environments. The influence of healthy, thriving leaders produces healthy, thriving environments. This is not only true in families and organizations but also in cities and nations. Jesus gave His church the mandate to disciple the nations.

> **Effective leaders have a hunger to grow and to become healthy spiritually, emotionally, and mentally.** ✑

None of us is perfect, but perfection is not a requirement to lead. Growth, however, is. Effective leaders have a hunger to grow and to become healthy spiritually, emotionally, and mentally. They understand that the environments they are called to influence need them to be as healthy as possible. So we must have a passion for growing healthy as we follow Jesus.

I have a passion to see believers grow as leaders. Leaders are part of God's brilliant plan to see cities and nations healed. The people I want to hang out with are those who have embraced the call to influence the world around them for God. I especially get excited about seeing healthy leaders raised up, because healthy leaders produce healthy environments.

Every healthy leader must establish two guardrails in their lives in order to create safe, healthy boundaries: Scripture and community. In chapters 11 and 12, I will address the topic of community more thoroughly, but Scripture is the other thing that keeps you on track in your growth as a leader. As the psalmist said, "Your word is a lamp to my feet and a light to my path" (119:105). The Word keeps us on the right path.

My challenge to you is to commit to getting your roots in the Word. These days it is easier than ever to get the Bible in you. The YouVersion Bible app lays out any number of reading plans and devotionals for you to use, and the app will send reminders to your devices to help you stick to your plan.

As a follower of Jesus, you cannot escape His mandate to disciple the nations. It is the call on your life. You have been given a measure of influence and placed on a team that is changing the world. You are called to use that influence to lead people into a place of blessing, strength, and health. Cities and nations are waiting for you to embrace your call to lead, and the place to start embracing it is in Scripture.

THREE SOILS

A thriving root system is built on trust and truth, which grow strong in our lives as we come to know God through His Word and through personal encounters with Him. However, in order to build our roots in trust and truth, God needs to plant our lives in various soils where we gain specific nutrients for growth. As I mentioned in chapter 1, God's process in David's life placed him into three different soils that developed the different dimensions of trust and truth in his life: the soil of intimacy, the soil of serving, and the soil of community. As you will see in the chapters ahead, each of these soils teaches us how to align our lives with God's truth and leads us to encounter God in different ways.

Soil 1

INTIMACY

7

Finding God

He who dwells in the secret place of
the Most High
Shall abide under the shadow of the
Almighty.

Psalm 91:1

My all-time favorite cookies are my mom's chocolate chip cookies. Without a doubt, they are the best cookies on the planet. Once when I was fifteen years old, I stayed home sick from school. I actually wasn't that sick, because by the middle of the day I was bored. So I told Mom that I wanted to make a batch of chocolate chip cookies. She said they were easy to make and told me where to find her recipe.

The recipe didn't look complicated. Everything seemed basic: eggs, sugar, butter, flour, chocolate chips, and vanilla. I had to hunt for the flour, but finally found a large Tupperware container filled with the powdery stuff and measured two cups of it into a bowl. When everything was mixed, I carefully spooned the batter onto a cookie sheet and slid it into the oven.

When I pulled my cookies out fifteen minutes later, they didn't look like Mom's. Hers were always light, fluffy, and round. Mine were dark brown, flat, big, and crunchy. I cautiously took a bite and spat it out. It tasted like pure salt.

When Mom came home, I said, "Your recipe doesn't work."

"What are you talking about? My recipe works fine."

"I followed your recipe to a T. It doesn't work. Look at my cookies."

She took a look at the brown discs and said, "Show me what you did."

I recited all the steps I had taken in order, showing her exactly where I had gotten each ingredient. When I held up the flour container, she shook her head.

"Banning, that's not flour."

"What is it?"

"That's baking soda."

I learned that day that cookies don't taste good when you substitute two cups of baking soda for flour.

Whatever goes in at the beginning—the foundation—matters greatly because it affects the outcome. God wants to build your foundation with the right ingredients and in the right order. Your root system, your inner world, is a personal relationship with Him marked by intimacy, dependence, faith, and rest. Where do you find those ingredients? You find them in the secret place of prayer. They are critical if you are to establish a healthy root system that produces lasting fruit.

As we saw, David's first move after being anointed king was to return to the field and his sheep. The field was the secret place where he built a foundation of intimacy with God that enabled him to thrive and ultimately fulfill God's purpose for his life. Building a secret-place lifestyle like David's is critical in our process with the Lord, because it is in our secret place that God meets with us and establishes the root system, the foundational elements, for the fruit that lasts.

> **It is in our secret place
> that God meets with us and
> establishes the root system,
> the foundational elements,
> for the fruit that lasts.**

As we intentionally draw near to God in prayer, two vital things develop in our root system. First, the priority of love becomes the motivation of our life. Second, God reveals to us the story He is unfolding on the earth and anoints us for the part we are to play in His plan.

ENCOUNTERING THE FATHER

Matthew 6:6 says, "But you, when you pray, go into your room, and when you have shut your door, pray to your Father who is in the secret place; and your Father who sees in secret will reward you openly." The first reason to develop a secret-place lifestyle is because we find God in the secret place. He is waiting there for us.

Finding God is paramount, because the first call on our lives is to *be with* God. When Jesus called His disciples, the first thing He wanted was for them to be with Him: "And He went up on the mountain and called to Him those He Himself wanted. And they came to Him. Then He appointed twelve, *that they might be with Him* and that He might send them out to preach, and to have power to heal sicknesses and to cast out demons" (Mark 3:13–15). Jesus's goal was not to pass information on to His disciples; it was to impart who He was and to reproduce Himself in them. Before Jesus ever sent the disciples, He first called them to be *with* Him. Jesus's strategy for raising up those who would take the gospel into all the world was to say, "Come be with Me. Let Me show you who I am and what I'm all about."

> **Everything you will ever need is found in the presence of God, for it is there you find the reason you were created.**

If this connection with Jesus is not developed in your life, your root system will never be healthy. You will never find satisfaction or experience what you were created for outside of encountering the presence of God. Everything you will ever need is found in the presence of God, for it is there you find the reason you were created.

Everything in your life must be birthed from the revelation of His love for you. God desires to draw close to you and reveal His love, which is better than life itself (see Psalm 63:3). This must be the first ingredient placed in your life.

The secret-place lifestyle of Jesus provoked the disciples to live in the same place of prayer. The disciples were constantly waking in the morning and discovering that Jesus was gone. He had stayed up all night praying, or He had awakened early and departed to a solitary place to pray. When they found Jesus in prayer, communing with His Father, it stirred something inside them to ask Him to teach them to pray (see Luke 11:1).

REVELATION OF FIRST LOVE

As you spend time with the Lord in your secret place, the things He cares about and the way He does things begin to rub off on you. You encounter His heart and His thoughts, which in turn shape how you live and think. He rearranges your priorities. The desire to make His name famous on the earth grows in passion and focus, while any desire to make a name for yourself fades away. You learn to be motivated solely by love for Him.

Those who become famous in their secret place are the ones who get to make Jesus famous on the earth. The real question is not whether you can be passionate when you are at a great worship service with thousands of others who love Jesus and your favorite worship team is leading. The question is whether your heart is alive with love for Him when you are all by yourself. It's in the inner room where you encounter His love for you, where your love for Him is ignited, and where a root system of love for God is born. David not only led from this place; he lived from this place.

> **It's in the inner room where you encounter His love for you, where your love for Him is ignited, and where a root system of love for God is born.** 🖋

When you stop living from your secret place, the temptation to be motivated by other things besides love for Jesus creeps in. Encountering His love for you in the secret place is what keeps your heart burning for your first love and keeps in place the priority of His presence. Be intentional about making sure your foundation is a life lived in the secret place with Jesus.

THE STRATEGY OF THE INNER ROOM

I highly value living passionately for God. Yet I often observe believers who are excited about the possibility of being used by God but who have no strategy attached to their zeal. As a leader, I see them frequently. They remind me of my son when I first taught him to play Yahtzee.

If you've never played Yahtzee, it's a simple game with five dice in a cup. With each turn of three dice rolls, you throw all or some of your dice, trying to achieve a good combination of numbers; different combinations mean different scores. While luck plays a big role in Yahtzee, strategy makes a difference. The roll called Yahtzee is worth the most points, but it's the hardest combination to get.

On every turn, Lake announced that he would roll for a Yahtzee. Turn after turn went by, and he never rolled a Yahtzee. Several times I tried to explain the strategy of the game. He seemed to listen intently to what I was saying, but when his turn came again, he just rolled all his dice and yelled "Yahtzee!"

Lake never won a game of Yahtzee. He had no strategy whatsoever for the game, but he did have lots of passion and zeal.

In the same way, I believe many Christians get excited about the idea of being used by God to change the world. They walk around with passion, yelling "Revival!" I love the passion to change the world, but we're not going to change anything by yelling "Yahtzee!" every time. We need a strategy attached to our passion.

The most strategic thing you can do with your life is to plant it in the secret place with God. We are not called simply to work for God; we are called to love God with everything within us. Jesus made this clear when He addressed Martha and told her that Mary was doing the more important thing (see Luke 10:42). If you want God to use your life, the most practical, strategic thing you can do is to establish it in the inner room of prayer. Allow the Lord to meet you in your secret place and develop your roots in hiding. It's important to have a history with the Lord that is hidden, that no one else knows about.

There are certain things God wants to release to you that He will only give you in the secret place. You can look in other places for them, but you won't find them. I recently read about a critically endangered bat on Silhouette Island, part of the Seychelles Archipelago in the Indian Ocean. These bats live nowhere else in the world. If you had a desire to see one, you could travel across Africa, look all over North and South America, and search all of Europe, but you wouldn't find a Seychelles sheath-tailed bat. You won't even find it on the other islands of the Seychelles. No matter how hard you look, you will only find this bat in one place: Silhouette Island. It's the same with finding certain things in God. There is an anointing that is found only in one place. You can go to as many conferences as you want, but you will not find it there. God reserves certain things to be found only in the secret place alone with Him. If you want to receive them, you have to separate yourself to the inner room of prayer.

THE ANOINTING OF JEHU

All the people who received a divine strategy from God had a key moment in which God encountered them and forever changed the trajectory of their lives. In the history of Israel, one of the most dramatic of such moments was the anointing of Jehu as king of Israel.

The years leading up to this moment were among the darkest in Israel's history. The reign of King Ahab and Queen Jezebel had unleashed unprecedented idolatry, sexual immorality, and violence in the nation. Elijah the prophet confronted Ahab and Jezebel on several occasions, but when the time came for God to take

Elijah to heaven, the royal couple was still in power. But God had promised Elijah that their family line would be removed in the next generation through Elisha, Elijah's successor, and Jehu, the man God had chosen to be king and to reestablish righteousness in the land.

When the time came for Jehu to be anointed king, Ahab was dead and his son had succeeded him, but Jezebel was still ruling the nation from Jezreel. Elisha sent one of the sons of the prophets to find Jehu in Ramoth Gilead, where he was stationed with some other soldiers:

> And Elisha the prophet called one of the sons of the prophets, and said to him, "Get yourself ready, take this flask of oil in your hand, and go to Ramoth Gilead. Now when you arrive at that place, look there for Jehu the son of Jehoshaphat, the son of Nimshi, and go in and make him rise up from among his associates, and take him to an inner room. Then take the flask of oil, and pour it on his head, and say, 'Thus says the LORD: "I have anointed you king over Israel."' Then open the door and flee, and do not delay."
>
> So the young man, the servant of the prophet, went to Ramoth Gilead. And when he arrived, there were the captains of the army sitting; and he said, "I have a message for you, Commander."
>
> Jehu said, "For which one of us?"
>
> And he said, "For you, Commander." Then he arose and went into the house. And he poured the oil on his head,

and said to him, "Thus says the LORD God of Israel:
'I have anointed you king over the people of the LORD,
over Israel. You shall strike down the house of Ahab your
master, that I may avenge the blood of My servants the
prophets, and the blood of all the servants of the LORD,
at the hand of Jezebel. For the whole house of Ahab shall
perish; and I will cut off from Ahab all the males in Israel,
both bond and free. So I will make the house of Ahab
like the house of Jeroboam the son of Nebat, and like
the house of Baasha the son of Ahijah. The dogs shall
eat Jezebel on the plot of ground at Jezreel, and there shall
be none to bury her." And he opened the door and fled.
(2 Kings 9:1–10)

When Jehu came out of this inner-room encounter, he told
his companions all that the prophet had spoken to him. They immediately rode to Jezreel, where they killed the kings of Israel and
Judah. At Jehu's command, Jezebel's attendants threw her out of a
window and she died. In one day the government that had done
such damage to the people of Israel was overthrown and a righteous government was established.

SEPARATED TO AN INNER ROOM

When the prophet arrived and asked Jehu to rise up from his as-
sociates and separate himself to an inner room, Jehu had no idea
that God was about to shift an entire nation on that day. After

being mired for decades in darkness, oppression, hopelessness, and discouragement, suffering under the hand of Jezebel, the story of Israel was about to take a huge, redemptive turn. And the first step in this process was that one man was about to encounter God and take action. In order for the message to be delivered, however, Jehu was required to stand up and separate himself to an inner room. Only then could God anoint him and speak to him a word that would change the nation's destiny.

God wants to speak to us about who He has called us to be and what He has called us to do, and to ignite a mandate on our lives, but what is required is separation to our inner room. The inner room is the place where we separate ourselves from everyone else and are alone with God. It's the place where God will give us the strategies and anointing to address the specific issues He has called us to address in our generation. For David, the inner room was the field. John the Baptist's inner room was the desert. Jesus chose His inner room wherever He could as He journeyed and ministered throughout Israel, regularly finding a lonely place to spend time with the Father.

The hour we live in requires of us a life given to the inner room. Everywhere we turn we hear talk about how bleak things are becoming. But men and women in the past and in the Bible faced similar situations. Jehu lived in one of the darkest hours in the history of Israel. But in the inner room he learned that God's heart was burdened for His people and that He had a plan to release them from their oppression. In the inner room, Jehu first captured the heart of the Father for the nation, and then he responded to the Father's invitation for him to play a role in His plan. In the same way, I know that we will see our nation shift as men and women of God begin to separate themselves to their inner room, receive His heart for our nation, and hear His word for them.

THE STORY OF GOD

Before Jehu entered the inner room, he had one understanding of the story of his nation and of what God was doing in the nation. When he came out of the inner room, he had an entirely different understanding of that story.

> **When you separate yourself to the inner room of prayer, the Lord begins to shift the narrative that's been shaping your perspective on your time and place in history.**

It's in the inner room of prayer that the Lord reveals His story to you. One of the things that grieves my heart is how many people don't know the story of God—past or present—in their life, city, region, or nation. When I talk to people, they aren't really sure what God is doing in the world. They don't know that God is on the move in the nations of the earth in an unprecedented way.

They don't know that He wants to invite them into His story, into what's happening in their city and nation. Do *you* know that He wants to invite you into His story in your city, in your nation?

When you separate yourself to the inner room of prayer, the Lord begins to shift the narrative that's been shaping your perspective on your time and place in history. You begin to see the story that's unfolding. He says, *I know right now what you see in the land isn't good, but I'm about to turn the tables and change everything. The story is about to get good.*

God is not only unfolding a story on the earth, but He is also active in your life with His story. He is writing His story over you. He has a plan and a purpose for your life that is full of hope and courage.

CLARITY

God not only reveals His story in the inner room; He also reveals in the inner room your unique role in that story. You have a critical part to play in the story of God on the earth, and that part becomes clear to you in the secret place. In order for you to play your part well, you must receive clarity about what your part is.

John the Baptist was prepared in the secret place of the desert. In the desert, he fasted, prayed, encountered the word of the Lord for his life, and became possessed by that word. When the Lord brought him out of the desert, he had stunning clarity about who he was and what he was called to do. When the religious leaders asked him if he was the Messiah, he answered them categorically:

Now this is the testimony of John, when the Jews sent priests and Levites from Jerusalem to ask him, "Who are you?"

He confessed, and did not deny, but confessed, "I am not the Christ."

And they asked him, "What then? Are you Elijah?"

He said, "I am not."

"Are you the Prophet?"

And he answered, "No."

Then they said to him, "Who are you, that we may give an answer to those who sent us? What do you say about yourself?"

He said: "I am

'The voice of one crying in the wilderness:
"Make straight the way of the Lord,"'

as the prophet Isaiah said." (John 1:19–23)

John the Baptist had no confusion over his part in the story. When people came with questions, he was clear: "*This* is who I am. *This* is my mandate. *This* is what God has called me to do. *This* is the story that's unfolding. *This* is the part I will play."

When God gives you this level of clarity about your part in His story and who you are, it brings great authority and focus to your life. Many people have no authority because they are confused as to who they are and what their role and assignment are in the story of God. God wants you to walk in so much authority and focus that you never waver from who you are. Part of the root system being developed in your life is this process of understanding what God is doing and what your assignment is.

HOPE

When you discover the story God is unfolding on the earth, it inevitably fills you with hope. It's hard to stay discouraged when you see that God is still on His throne and is carrying out a master plan to bring all things under His rule and reign. Psalm 29:10 says, "The LORD sat enthroned at the Flood, and the LORD sits as King forever." The same God who reshaped the world through the Flood is the same God who is shaping history today. Seeing this truth ignites hope in our hearts and creates expectation to see God move.

In 1904 a revival occurred in Wales that has shaped the church around the world. Many denominations and churches trace their roots back to the influence of this early twentieth-century outpouring. The revival was led by twenty-six-year-old Evan Roberts. For twelve years, from ages fourteen to twenty-six, he established a secret-place lifestyle with the Lord. He was in the Word and in prayer. He separated himself, and the Lord spoke to him in those years about the revival that was coming. His encounters in the secret place awakened his heart to the hope of national transformation. As a result, his prayers of great faith moved heaven.

We need an entire generation awake to what God can do and all the possibilities that flow from His ability. We are often more aware of what the Enemy can do than what God can do. We need to stop being impressed with darkness. We need to find out what God intends to do in our lifetime. And we need to become impressed with that. When the Lord begins to show you what is possible, faith and hope are released into your life and instill fresh conviction in your prayers, which ultimately moves the heart of God.

> **We need an entire generation awake to what God can do and all the possibilities that flow from His ability.**

Sometimes in prayer meetings I can tell that no one is praying with conviction. It's clear that the people praying don't know who they are in God. Their prayers feel dutiful and halfhearted. It sounds good to say, *God, change my city.* But when the Lord speaks to you in the inner room, you move from halfhearted prayers to passionate, wholehearted cries: *God, You told me You'd awaken an entire generation in my nation! You said that entire cities could be saved, that we would see transformation!* You begin to intensely focus on and feel passionate about what He spoke to you, not only for your city and nation, but for your life.

Do you know who changes nations? People who are driven by a word from God. If you want to become driven by the word of the Lord for your life, then you need to intentionally, deliberately commit to the inner room. That is where God wants to develop your life and bring clarity, authority, and focus to your role in His story. Lasting fruit that brings change to the world starts in the inner room of prayer.

8

What to Do When You're Expecting

My eyes are awake through the night
watches,
That I may meditate on Your word.

Psalm 119:148

I f you have had kids, you are undoubtedly familiar with the ritual of pregnancy tests. I have three children, so my wife and I have done this ritual more than once. Each time, we went to a store, bought the test, came back to the house, and SeaJay went in the bathroom to take the test. We made small talk about our day as we waited for the stick to do its thing. Finally, we looked at it.

If the test had one line, it meant she wasn't pregnant. One line meant that life continued as normal. But if there were two lines, life as we knew it would never be the same. In only three minutes, our lives had changed. SeaJay looked and felt exactly as she had before those three minutes, but upon seeing a second line, our priorities shifted, and we moved into full-on preparation mode. We started scheduling appointments, painting rooms, buying things, and thinking about names—all because of a second line.

When you plant yourself in the inner room of prayer, you will encounter the Lord speaking to you. When the Lord speaks to you, it is like seeing a second line on a pregnancy test. He's telling you that you're pregnant and that it's time to start preparing for that word to come to pass. When you're pregnant with a baby, you can be sure that it's coming in nine months—ready or not. When you're pregnant with a word from the Lord, it might be months, years, or decades before the word comes full term and you can deliver it, but you have a responsibility to carry that word until then. How you carry that word matters greatly. Many people get tripped up in the process of God because they don't know how to carry what God has spoken to them.

In 1 Samuel 1, Hannah desperately cried out to the Lord for a son. Nothing else would satisfy her, even a husband who was extremely good to her. She was pressing for a son and would settle for nothing less. As she was crying out in front of the temple, Eli, the high priest, saw her and thought she was drunk. But when he scolded her for being drunk at the temple, she said, "No, my lord, I am a woman of sorrowful spirit. I have drunk neither wine nor intoxicating drink, but have poured out my soul before the LORD" (verse 15). At that moment, Eli gave her what she needed—a word from the Lord: "Go in peace, and the God of Israel grant your petition which you have asked of Him" (verse 17).

Many times we're pressing in for things, and the Lord doesn't give us what we're asking for at first. Instead, He gives us a word. After receiving this word from Eli, Hannah got up and shifted her focus: "So [Hannah] went her way and ate, and her face was no longer sad" (verse 18). She hadn't received a child; she received a *word*. Her husband couldn't heal her grief, but a word from God changed everything for her. Hannah was pregnant with a word before she was pregnant with a son. Nothing changed for her physically, but she had a word, and that's all she needed. Hannah got up and began to carry the word.

Jesus made a tremendous promise in John 15:7. He said, "If you abide in Me, and My words abide in you, you will ask what you desire, and it shall be done for you." Asking what you desire and seeing God do it for you is called *faith*. Faith gets an answer from God. But faith is connected to something—the words of Christ abiding in you. What does that mean?

If we take a look at the original language, we find that the Greek word translated "words" is *rhema*, which means "that which is or has been uttered by the living voice."[*] The words of Jesus include what He *has said* and what He *is saying*. The word "abide" is the Greek word *men o*, which means "to be held, kept, continually."[†] Putting this all together, we see that the realm of faith is accessed first by drawing close to Jesus and hearing Him—for faith comes by hearing (see Romans 10:17)—both through what He has spoken in Scripture and through what He is speaking today.

---

[*] James Strong, *Strong's Exhaustive Concordance of the Bible* (Peabody, MA: Hendrikson, 1980), G4487.

[†] Strong, *Exhaustive Concordance*, G3306.

But it's not enough to just hear the Lord's words; we must carry them. We must hold and keep His words at all times and allow them to abide in us. Carrying His words is what shapes our desires and our prayers so we get answers from God. Carrying His words is what gives us access to faith.*

> The realm of faith is accessed first by drawing close to Jesus and hearing Him—for faith comes by hearing—both through what He has spoken in Scripture and through what He is speaking today. 🖋

Rich Dad, Poor Dad† is a great book on finances and economics. The author's premise is that the American education system doesn't educate people on what to do with money. His point is that everyone wants more money, but if we get it, we don't really know what to do with it. Therefore, what we need is not more money but an education on what to do with money so that we will

---

* Scripture is the final authority, and our ability to hear God speaking to us is connected to our roots being firmly anchored in Scripture. God is not speaking in a way that supersedes His written Word or that adds to it, but He is speaking to us in a variety of ways.

† See Robert T. Kiyosaki, *Rich Dad, Poor Dad: What the Rich Teach Their Kids About Money—That the Poor and Middle Class Do Not!* (New York: Warner Business Books, 2000).

know what to do when we receive money instead of mismanaging it and ending up in the same place. This is very similar when it comes to receiving a word from the Lord. A lot of people want a word from the Lord, but they don't need a word from the Lord—they need to know what to do with the words they already have. So let's look at some practical things we should do to carry the word and let it abide in our lives.

Pray It

The first way you carry the word of the Lord is by praying it. This may seem simple and obvious, but I'm continually surprised by people who don't realize that when the Lord speaks, they must carry what He is saying in prayer. Or perhaps they prayed for a season but eventually laid down the word and no longer carried it in prayer. The word has to become fuel for your prayer life.

I think we are to do more than just pray "over" things. I think we should use Christ's *rhema*—both what He has said and is saying—to pray about them. I don't pray over my finances, children, nation, and future; I pray what He has said about my finances, children, nation, and future.

Years ago a friend and I decided to work with a contractor who buys houses in need of repair and fixes them up to sell. Our job was to look at the public records of houses in foreclosure, find ones that fit certain criteria, and then bid on those houses at the courthouse. We did the research and made a list of the houses we wanted to bid on. When we got to the courthouse, however, we were outbid on every house on our list. Then a home came up on the foreclosure list that we hadn't heard about and hadn't done any research on. It was in our price range and seemed like a great deal, so we bought it.

Within fifteen minutes of purchasing this property, we learned that we actually owed an amount four times greater than what we had paid. Very quickly we realized that was just the beginning of the craziness. We encountered obstacle after obstacle as we attempted to prepare the house for resale. It took two years and a lot more money than we had planned to spend before we finally sold what was supposed to be a quick flip.

One night during this two-year process, I felt so overwhelmed I could not sleep. I got up, grabbed my Bible, and headed into our walk-in closet to get before the Lord. There I read the prayer of David in Psalm 28:1–2:

> Do not be silent to me,
> Lest, if You are silent to me,
> I become like those who go down to the pit.
> Hear the voice of my supplications
> When I cry to You,
> When I lift up my hands toward Your holy sanctuary.

I began to pray, *Lord, I need You not to be silent to me right now. I need You to talk to me.*

The Lord began to speak to me in that closet not only about that situation but also about my finances for the rest of my life. The circumstances did not change during my time in the closet, but the Lord had talked to me. From that point on, whenever stress arose because of the property, I would pray what He spoke to me. And since that time, the Lord has reminded me to pray what He said in that closet over my finances.

One of the things I'm constantly pressing in to hear from the Lord is what He is saying about my children. Before they were born, each of my kids had people who prayed over them and spoke about their destiny. We actually picked names for them according to what had been prayed over them. In fact, you could say that my children's names *are* prayers. They are a way of saying back to God and to them what God said about who He has created and called them to be.

My first daughter's name is Ellianna, which is Hebrew for "My God has answered me." It's a feminine form of Elijah. The prayer over her life was that she would be a voice for the Lord, and she is. She has a beautiful sensitivity to Him.

When my second daughter was in the womb, someone prayed over her that she would be an evangelist poured out for an end-time harvest, and the person quoted Joel 2:23–24: "And He will cause the rain to come down for you—the former rain, and the latter rain in the first month. The threshing floors shall be full of wheat, and the vats shall overflow with new wine and oil." SeaJay also felt strongly that we were to name her "Friend of God." As a result, her first name is Raya, which is Hebrew for "Friend of God," and her middle name is Rain in reference to the passage from Joel. Raya is our little evangelist. She has such a heart for people. She's the one who finds the person in the room who nobody is talking to and immediately makes the person feel loved and valued. She makes us buy gift cards so that when we see somebody who's looking for food, we can give that person a restaurant gift card. If you are broken at all, Raya will find you and love you.

Before we knew whether our third child was a boy or girl, a friend called and said, "This may seem random, but I felt like the Lord brought the name Asa to mind this morning while I was praying for your next child."

I said, "I appreciate that, but I don't know if we're having a boy or girl, and if we have a boy, I'm not naming him Asa."

Shortly after that we went in for a sonogram and found out we were having a boy. I wanted to name him Lake, after John G. Lake, a minister of the early 1900s, and Wesley, which is my middle name. But we decided we would look up what Asa means. It's Hebrew, and it means "healer." We knew we couldn't ignore that, so I had to take back my statement that I would not name my son Asa. My son's full name is Wesley Asa Lake Liebscher.

CHANGE THE WAY YOU TALK

The second way you carry the word of the Lord is to change the way you talk. Again, this may seem elementary, but it's not something we pay a lot of attention to. Many times we say things He's not saying. Our language needs to line up with God's language. When the Lord speaks, we no longer have permission to say anything but what He has said.

I see a lot of people who hear God speaking to them about His incredible value and purpose for their lives—their identity, calling, family, finances, or career. But their language does not line up with what He has said. The Bible is very clear about what

God thinks of us and the plans He has for us. But for many of us, it does not change the way we talk. We still allow our feelings to be what we speak from rather than what God has said.

The promises of God for your life may not have fully manifested yet. You may not be able to see them with your eyes. But if that's what He has spoken over you, then that's what you are. And you need to change the way you talk about your life so that it aligns with what He says.

One night I asked a staffer to close worship at a conference session with prayer. She was nervous and hesitant at first, but she did it. Afterward I asked her how she thought it had gone.

"Oh, it wasn't that good," she said anxiously. "I felt like I was just stumbling around. I don't think anybody was impacted."

"Whoa," I responded. "How do you think Jesus sees your prayer?"

"I don't know," she admitted.

"You have five minutes to walk over there and figure it out. Then come back here."

> **Do you know what's more real than what you're looking at or feeling? What He said.**

She returned a few minutes later, smiling. I asked her what had happened.

"The Lord spoke to my heart and said my prayer was powerful and people's lives were impacted and He really enjoyed it."

On our team, we challenge people to say only what He is

saying. When we hear people saying things that God has not said, we challenge them to be alone with God and find out what He is saying. Once you hear what He's saying, you have to line up your language with His language. That's all you get to talk about, the only thing you're allowed to say. Your feelings can be inconsistent, but God's word never is. Change the way you talk, and challenge other people to change the way they talk. It doesn't feel real sometimes, but we walk by faith, not by sight. Do you know what's more real than what you're looking at or feeling? What He said.

MAKE IT THE MAIN THING

The next thing you have to do to carry the word of the Lord is to make it the main thing, make it your central focus. The word of the Lord can't be some side issue you pop in and out of. Can you imagine taking a pregnancy test and then thinking the pregnancy would be just a side issue in our lives:

> Four months later, at the dinner table, I suddenly remember SeaJay taking the test and ask, "Didn't you have a pregnancy test?"
>
> "That's right! That was amazing. That was really cool, wasn't it?"
>
> "Yeah, it was really awesome."
>
> "Okay, we'll talk about it later."

No way! When you take a pregnancy test, it's all you're going to talk about for a long time. *Trust me.* Every day you're talking about the growing baby who's about to show up in your life. It's not some side issue.

My dad was a police officer for thirty years. One of his partners was shot three times while pursuing a suspect into an apartment complex. He recovered, and sometime later I went to lunch with him. I was in my early twenties and extremely curious to hear what it was like to be shot. My first question right after we sat down was "What was it like being shot?"

He told me about the crazy things your body does in high-pressure, survival situations. He said that many times you don't bleed much externally because your body starts to shut down things that aren't necessary. It will shut down the more external blood paths and only send blood to the internal organs. Many times your brain slows things down and turns off your hearing and peripheral vision if they are not needed in that moment, so you can see only what you need to survive.

As the Lord often does with me, He used that as an object lesson for my spiritual life. The Lord spoke to my heart: *Banning, that's what I'm doing in your life. I'm going to start shutting down things that are not needed. I'm going to turn off peripheral vision and give you tunnel vision to see what I want you to see.* God wanted me to shut down things that didn't matter, that weren't main things. He wanted me to lock in on what He was doing, and He was going to help me to do that.

The word of the Lord is not something you visit every once in a while. It's to be the thing you are carrying, keeping, and holding close to you at all times. Only when the word abides in you will it come to full term and fulfillment.

Prepare for It

The last way you carry the word and allow it to abide or remain in you is to prepare for it. A story in 2 Kings 4 gives us an interesting illustration of this kind of preparation. Elisha encountered a widow who was about to sell her sons into slavery to pay off a debt. She cried out to Elisha, and he asked her what else she had. She told him she had a jar of oil. He then instructed her to gather from her neighbors as many containers as she could and to bring them into her house:

> So she went from him and shut the door behind her and her sons, who brought the vessels to her; and she poured [the oil] out. Now it came to pass, when the vessels were full, that she said to her son, "Bring me another vessel."
> And he said to her, "There is not another vessel."
> So the oil ceased. (verses 5–6)

The oil ceased on the last vessel, which leaves us to wonder: if they had had more containers, would there have been more oil?

I believe that our level of preparation determines our level of outpouring. It's not that it's dependent on our works, but we are involved in what God wants to do. We don't sit back and do nothing. Faith is active and alive, and when we believe God, we begin to prepare for what He tells us to prepare for.

You have to kick into preparation mode. No matter how small it may seem, you should be putting your hands to something. I will ask people, "What is the Lord telling you? What are you doing about it?" These conversations go something like this:

"The Lord told me I'm going to impact Latin America."
"So what are you doing about that?"
"I'm taking a Spanish class at a community college."

"The Lord told me I'm going to write books that are going to change the way the church thinks."
"What are you doing about it?"
"I started a blog."

"The Lord told me I'm going to have influence in education."
"What are you doing about that?"
"I'm researching schools that offer a master's degree in teaching."

"The Lord told me I'm going to improve the economy in third-world nations by investing in small businesses."
"What are you doing about that?"
"I'm reading about micro-lending and other successful small-business strategies."

Sometimes people admit they're not really doing anything to prepare for the word they've received from God. I've noticed several reasons for their failure to prepare. The first is that they don't really believe the word. I can tell whether or not someone believes a word they've received by what they're doing or not doing. How do we know that Noah believed God? He started building an ark. How do we know Hannah believed Him? Because she stopped crying and went home expecting a son.

Second, they don't want to do things that feel small compared to the size of the task Christ laid before them. It's as though they feel things are beneath them or not worth their time. They don't understand that the small things they are being faithful with are their faith in action. The small things are preparation as you move toward what God has called you to do.

Third, they may be crippled with indecision. They don't want to make a wrong decision, so they make no decision. But no decision is always the wrong decision. I remember watching a show on survival in the wilderness. One of the main points was that if you are lost, you must make a decision and go with it. Many people don't ever make it out of the wilderness because they are so scared of making a wrong decision that they never make any decision. God can't direct you when you're staying put.

> **The difference between people who do something and people who don't do something is that the people who do something actually *do* something.**

The simple truth is you need to engage with what God has spoken to you. I've wondered over the years why some people make a difference and some don't. I finally realized that the difference between people who do something and people who don't do something is that the people who do something actually *do* something. They don't make excuses. They don't say, "That's below me." Instead, they position themselves for what God said and go for it.

Fear of failure is a big thing. For some reason, we believe that failure is the worst possible outcome, and therefore we set our lives up to never fail. We think that if we step out and what we do doesn't work, we won't be able to handle it. "I have a dream of starting a prayer movement in my city. But what if I start a prayer meeting and nobody shows up? I don't think I could handle that. It would be too embarrassing." So we don't do anything, and we miss what God has for us.

In the parable of the talents, Jesus compared three servants who had been entrusted by their master with some money to manage. Two of the servants invested the money, but one buried it. When his master asked him why he hadn't invested it like the other two, he said, "I was afraid" (Matthew 25:25). How did the master respond? He was not happy. He hadn't lost his money, but he had discovered that his servant's fear of failure made the servant useless. He fired the servant and gave his money to another who was willing to use what they had been given, even if it meant risking its loss.

The message of this parable is that setting up our lives not to fail is, in fact, failing. The only way we can truly fail as sons and daughters of God is to refuse to use what He's given us. When we take risks to use what He's given us or to do what He's asked of us, we are successful, even when we don't get the results we expect, because we are acting like true sons and daughters who actually believe their Dad when He speaks to them.

My pastor told me, "The difference between the men and women of God who made an impact on history and those who didn't is that those who made an impact weren't afraid to fail for God."

Go after the things God has spoken to you, even if it's scary. Don't let the fear of failure paralyze you from acting on what God has said. You aren't as fragile as you think you are. Things may not work out exactly as you planned, but you are moving forward, refusing to stay neutral to what He has spoken to your heart. You are being a true son or daughter of your Father, and there is no greater success than that.

ROOTS OF INTIMACY

In order for God to prepare you to carry the full weight of long-term fruit, He has to establish your root system in intimacy with Him. He needs to plant you in a soil where He can get your full attention, ignite a love for Him that becomes your primary motivation, speak to you about your calling and mandate, and lead you as you carry out those words—and that soil is the field of intimacy. If you want your roots of trust and truth to grow deep and strong, you must, like David and Jesus, establish a secret-place lifestyle in the midst of God's process.

Soil 2

SERVING

9

An Unlikely Marriage

Ahimelek answered the king, "Who of all
your servants is as loyal as David, the king's
son-in-law, captain of your bodyguard and
highly respected in your household?"

1 Samuel 22:14, NIV

A long with preparing David for the throne in the *soil of intimacy,* God prepared David in the *soil of serving.* After being anointed by Samuel, David not only continued to serve in his father's house by caring for the sheep and taking food to his brothers on the front lines of a war, but he was also called upon by Saul to serve as his personal worship leader and armor bearer (see 1 Samuel 16:14–23). David didn't embrace this position of serving Saul merely because he thought it might be a steppingstone to the throne; he maintained an attitude of humility and service even when Saul turned against him. He sacrificed opportunity after opportunity to reach out and take what God had promised him, choosing instead to honor and serve a man who often tried to take his life.

David's choice to serve the man in power, rather than opposing him, was a critical element in his root system. It not only was an incredible expression of his trust in God, a commitment to let God fulfill the word over his life in His way and His time, but it also revealed that David understood something about what it meant to be the Lord's anointed one. Unlike Saul, David recognized that this position of power was, in fact, a position of great responsibility and accountability. It was a position of serving. And thus David prepared for this huge role of public service by serving both the One who created that role and the one currently in that role.

Jesus's School of Identity

David's choice to embrace serving as the appropriate role for a would-be king was a foreshadowing of Christ, the true and eternal Servant King. But it is also a model for us, because as the Bible tells us, we not only follow Christ, but we are *in* Christ. Colossians 2:9–10 says, "For in [Jesus] dwells all the fullness of the Godhead bodily; and you are complete in Him, who is the head of all principality and power." Being in Christ means that we share His identity and position and, therefore, must learn to carry ourselves as He does.

These two revelations continually must grow together in our lives: the revelation of who He is and the revelation of who we are *in* Him. In the Gospels, we see that Jesus led His disciples deeper into the revelation of who He was and who they were in Him. This revelation had at least three dimensions. The disciples received the *revelation of greatness,* the *revelation of leadership,* and the *revelation of royalty.*

I was raised in churches where we did not believe we had any greatness in us. But Jesus raised His disciples to believe the opposite. He kept setting them up to discover that He was putting greatness on them. Luke 9 contains an amazing progression of some of these setups: First, in verses 1–6, Jesus deputized His disciples to carry His power and authority, then sent them out to preach and heal. Next, in verses 12–17, He involved them in the miracle of the feeding of the five thousand. Then Peter, James, and John had the jaw-dropping encounter on the mountain with a transfigured Jesus talking with Moses and Elijah, and hearing God's voice from heaven in verses 28–36.

> You *are* called to greatness.
> But greatness looks different
> than you think. If you really
> want to be great, here's how
> you do it: become the least. ✍

Not too long after these incredible experiences, what happened? "Then a dispute arose among them as to which of them would be greatest" (verse 46). Jesus's disciples were wondering who would be greatest because Jesus created around Himself an environment where they received a revelation of their greatness in Him. And Jesus didn't burst their bubble. He didn't say, "You're not really great. Only God is great." Instead He said, "He who is least among you all will be great" (verse 48). In other words, Jesus said, "You *are* called to greatness. But greatness looks different than you think. If you really want to be great, here's how you do it: become the least."

We see the same pattern and progression in the revelation of leadership. When the seventy disciples returned from their mission trip, they told Jesus, "Lord, even the demons are subject to us in Your name" (Luke 10:17). They were exploding with excitement over the revelation of the authority Jesus had put on their lives. Jesus didn't say, "Well, don't get too excited. I was just lending you My authority so you could take care of some of My business." No, He said, "Behold, I give you the authority to trample on serpents and scorpions, and over all the power of the enemy, and nothing shall by any means hurt you" (verse 19). However, He showed them the proper attitude toward their authority by explaining which aspect of it they were to get excited about: "Nevertheless do not rejoice in this, that the spirits are subject to you, but rather rejoice because your names are written in heaven" (verse 20).

Lastly, the disciples received the revelation of royalty as Jesus showed them what it looked like to be the true Son of the King. If there was ever a more upside-down revelation for the disciples, this had to be it. First, Jesus completely blew up the idea of God as a benevolent dictator, revealing Him instead as a Father of radical love who expects His sons and daughters to be like Him:

> You have heard that it was said, "You shall love your
> neighbor and hate your enemy." But I say to you, love

your enemies, bless those who curse you, do good to those
who hate you, and pray for those who spitefully use you
and persecute you, *that you may be sons of your Father
in heaven;* for He makes His sun rise on the evil and on
the good, and sends rain on the just and on the unjust. . . .
Therefore you shall be perfect, just as your Father in
heaven is perfect. (Matthew 5:43–45, 48)

Next, Jesus totally flipped their understanding of how members of His royal family were to relate to leading. In their world,
there was only one way for kings to behave—kings set up their
lives to be served. The Israelites knew that the king could call on
them or their children to serve at any time. The king's people paid
taxes to serve his needs. Jesus's version of royalty was the opposite:

But Jesus called [the disciples] to Himself and said, "You
know that the rulers of the Gentiles lord it over them,
and those who are great exercise authority over them.
Yet it shall not be so among you; but whoever desires to
become great among you, let him be your servant. And
whoever desires to be first among you, let him be your
slave—just as the Son of Man did not come to be served,
but to serve, and to give His life a ransom for many."
(Matthew 20:25–28)

Jesus forever married the concepts of greatness, leadership,
and royalty with the concepts of humility, love, and service. These
are the three upside-down revelations of who Jesus is and who we

are in Him. He is great and we are great in Him—but that greatness is expressed by becoming the least. He is a leader and we are leaders in Him—but our joy as leaders who carry His authority is not in conquest; instead, our joy is in the One who chose us to represent Him. He is royalty, the true Son of the King, and we are royal sons and daughters in Him—but we look like our father and our elder brother by demonstrating radical love and service. As we step into the revelation of who we are in Him, we must cling to His example and never revert to the world's versions of greatness, leadership, and royalty, which turn humility into pride, authority into domination, and love into self-serving.

THE GREATEST LOVE

The greatest love, Jesus famously declared, was to lay down your life for others: "Greater love has no one than this, than to lay down one's life for his friends" (John 15:13). Jesus not only said it; He did it. He demonstrated the greatest love by laying down His life for us.

Most people innately understand that there is no greater act of selflessness than laying down one's life for others. Americans, like people of other countries, give great honor for the military and celebrate them on multiple holidays throughout the year, because we recognize there's no greater sacrifice than theirs—laying down their lives for the rest of us. Many *have* paid the highest price, and the rest are *willing* to pay that price.

A few years ago we did a Jesus Culture tour in the Pacific, with events in Malaysia, Singapore, Australia, and New Zealand.

My family came on the tour with me. By the time we arrived in the last city on our tour, Auckland, I was exhausted. So instead of sightseeing with the rest of our crew, I asked Lake, my son, if he wanted to relax and go see a movie with me. He said yes, so we headed to the theater and decided to see *Captain America*.

Toward the end of the movie is a scene in which Captain America falls off a ship and sinks into the darkness, apparently dead.

"Dad," Lake whispered, "that's the best way to die."

"What do you mean?" I asked.

"To die for your country," he stated confidently.

At his words, a wave of gratitude and patriotic pride washed over me. I wanted to stand up right there in that theater in New Zealand and start singing, "And I'm proud to be an American!" I also absolutely loved that Lake had grasped the power and value of sacrifice for something greater than himself.

But when Jesus told us to demonstrate the greatest love by laying down our lives, He wasn't referring just to our dying for something. He didn't lay down just His life by going to the cross. While Jesus paid that greatest price on our behalf, He also laid down His life every day through sacrificial service. Jesus served *everybody,* and He served them in ways that revealed He truly loved them.

The way Jesus served people had to blow the minds of His disciples. Again and again they would find their leader, the promised Messiah and King who was to defeat the enemies of Israel, serving people no respectable Jewish man of His day would even approach. He talked to an outcast Samaritan woman at a well,

stopped to have lunch with a hated tax collector, and touched un-
clean lepers. He served children, women, prostitutes, foreigners,
Roman soldiers, and beggars alike.

> **Love looks like serving. If we
> want to abide in Jesus's love,
> then we must embrace His
> lifestyle of serving people.** 🖉

Then, just before He went to the cross, Jesus told His disciples
that they were to serve one another as He had served them, and
He gave them an unforgettable lesson to show them what He
meant: He took the role of a servant and washed their feet. Peter's
reaction to Jesus's kneeling down with a towel around His waist
gives us a clue as to how crazy the disciples thought this was: "You
shall never wash my feet!" (John 13:8). You might think that after
three years of breaking their cultural boxes, Jesus wouldn't be able
to do something Peter would find so offensive—but He did. Then
He explicitly told them, "This is what I want you to do."

> So when He had washed their feet, taken His garments,
> and sat down again, He said to them, "Do you know
> what I have done to you? You call Me Teacher and Lord,
> and you say well, for so I am. If I then, your Lord and
> Teacher, have washed your feet, you also ought to wash
> one another's feet. For I have given you an example, that
> you should do as I have done to you. Most assuredly, I say

to you, a servant is not greater than his master; nor is he
who is sent greater than he who sent him." (verses 12–16)

Later in this discourse, Jesus followed up His command for
the disciples to serve one another as He had served them with an
additional command:

> As the Father loved Me, I also have loved you; abide in
> My love. . . .
> These things I have spoken to you, that My joy may
> remain in you, and that your joy may be full. This is My
> commandment, that you love one another as I have loved
> you. (John 15:9–12)

This progression from "Do as I have done to you" to "Love
one another as I have loved you" is Jesus's revelation of what true
love, the greatest love, looks like. *Love looks like serving.* If we
want to abide in Jesus's love, then we must embrace His lifestyle of
serving people.

How We Love Him

In the parable of the sheep and the goats, Jesus explained that
when we serve others He actually counts it as serving Him:

> "For I was hungry and you gave Me food; I was thirsty
> and you gave Me drink; I was a stranger and you took Me

in; I was naked and you clothed Me; I was sick and you
visited Me; I was in prison and you came to Me."

Then the righteous will answer Him, saying, "Lord,
when did we see You hungry and feed You, or thirsty and
give You drink? When did we see You a stranger and take
You in, or naked and clothe You? Or when did we see You
sick, or in prison, and come to You?" And the King will
answer and say to them, "Assuredly, I say to you, inasmuch
as you did it to one of the least of these My brethren, you
did it to Me." (Matthew 25:35–40)

Why does Jesus tell us to serve "the least"? Well, for one, serving those who can give us nothing in return has a pretty good
chance of being an act of true, sacrificial love. We imitate the sacrificial love of Christ when we serve the poor, outcasts, and crimi-
nals (see Luke 14:12–14). For another, serving the least is the only
way to *become* the least, which Jesus told us is the path to greatness.
The only way to get lower than the lowest is to serve them.

> **You simply cannot
> love Jesus and live
> for Him without
> loving people.** ✎

Serving and laying down your life for others is critical because
Jesus takes it personally. He says, "If you want to love Me, here's
how you do it: visit Me when I'm in prison. Clothe Me when I'm
naked. Feed Me when I'm hungry." We manifest our love for Him

by serving others. You simply cannot love Jesus and live for Him without loving people.

Sometimes people say, "It's not about you; it's about others." That's not wrong, but it doesn't go far enough. I don't think it's even about others; it's about Jesus. It's *all* about Him. We're about others because we're about Him. The reason we love, serve, and lay our lives down for other people is because that's what He has asked of us. He says that when we do those things, we're doing them to Him.

THANKLESS AND SATISFIED

Two things will reveal that we are beginning to understand who God is and who we are in Him as we step into the greatness, leadership, and royalty God has placed on our lives.

The first is that we look for opportunities to love and serve people. We increase our capacity to love and serve. In general, the opportunities for serving that you should be looking for are those that are nearby. The people closest to you should feel loved and served by you. If you're married, your love and service should be directed at your spouse and children. If you're not married, it should be directed toward your family and friends. God has placed these people in your lives so you can learn to love Him, become His friend, and step into the fullness of the greatness, leadership, and royalty you share in Him. He also wants to bless you so you can serve more effectively. Bill Johnson, senior pastor of Bethel Church in Redding, California, has always said, "Any increased blessing in your life is so that you can better serve others."

The second thing that reveals our understanding is that as we love and serve, our attitude and motivation are defined by one goal: we want to love Jesus.

Jesus addressed the attitude of a good and faithful servant in a profound story He told His disciples:

> And which of you, having a servant plowing or tending
> sheep, will say to him when he has come in from the field,
> "Come at once and sit down to eat"? But will he not rather
> say to him, "Prepare something for my supper, and gird
> yourself and serve me till I have eaten and drunk, and
> afterward you will eat and drink"? Does he thank that
> servant because he did the things that were commanded
> him? I think not. So likewise you, when you have done
> all those things which you are commanded, say, "We are
> unprofitable servants. We have done what was our duty to
> do." (Luke 17:7–10)

When I first studied this parable, it threw me off. Maybe it's because my top love language is words of affirmation, but it kind of irritated me when Jesus said, "Does he thank that servant because he did the things that were commanded him? I think not. So likewise you, when you have done all those things which you are commanded, say, 'We are unprofitable servants. We have done what was our duty to do.'" What did that mean? Is God telling us we shouldn't expect any thanks or praise for our service?

As I dug deeper, I saw that Jesus wasn't saying that good servants don't deserve thanks and praise. In the parable of the talents, for example, we see the master, who represents God, praising his servants: "Well done, good and faithful servant" (Matthew 25:21, 23). Jesus was addressing the attitude and motivation of good and faithful servants. Good servants don't serve *for* thanks and praise, and they don't *need* thanks and praise.

I've been around a lot of believers (and I've been one myself) who say "I've been working so hard in the children's ministry, and nobody even notices or thanks me" or "I've been stacking chairs and no one said thanks." There are countless other areas inside and outside the church walls where we look for thanks. Now, I want a grateful church, and I want all of our leaders to be appreciative of everybody who's serving. But at the end of the day, our service should be a gift we give to God. When we're serving God, we don't care if other people notice. We don't need them to thank us. We want to love Him. He told us the way to love Him was to serve, so that's what we're doing and why we're doing it. We serve as a gift to Him, not to be seen by others.

> **All of our lives should be about service and love to God through service and love to people.** ✒

All of our lives should be about service and love to God through service and love to people, and our attitude should be, "I'm doing what You commanded me to do. You told me I would be Your friend if I did what You commanded—to love people like

You love me. You've loved me radically, passionately, and zealously. You laid Your life down on the cross for me. The least I can do is go love other people like You loved me. I don't need a thankyou. If stacking chairs is serving people, then that's what I want to do."

When this is our attitude, then whether we receive thanks and praise from people or not, we can be satisfied with our offering. In fact, we know the praise and thanks of people won't satisfy us, because they're not the One we're trying to please. What satisfies us is when we get in the secret place and hear the Lord say, *I'm so pleased with you. I love how you love people, how you make people feel cared for, seen, valued, and known. I love how you lay your life down. Thank you for loving My body, especially those who don't often get loved. I love that there has been an increase of blessings in many areas in your life and that you're wondering, "How can I use this to serve other people?"* That's what we need to hear and whom we need to hear it from.

10

The Divine Exchange

David came to Saul and entered his service.

1 Samuel 16:21, NIV

When Jesus told His disciples that becoming least would lead to greatness, He also let them know they could expect rewards from embracing a lifestyle of serving. Obviously our core motivation for serving is to love and please Jesus—He is our "very great reward" (Genesis 15:1, NIV). But serving leads to our getting more of Him in our lives, and the Bible spells out what that looks like. While we could fill many books exploring the rewards of serving, we will look at four big ones here: grace, joy, safety, and promotion.

GRACE

When you position your life to serve, you take a posture of humility, and humility releases grace into your life. "God resists the proud," the Bible says, "but gives grace to the humble" (James 4:6).

Grace—the unmerited favor and operational power of God—is
the reward of humble service.

Contrary to what many people mistakenly believe, humble
service does not mean neglecting your own interests or needs. Lots
of people tell me they have become burned out on serving. When
I ask why, I usually discover that they have problems in taking
care of themselves and setting healthy boundaries in their lives—
signs that they struggle to value themselves and are looking for
value and identity through serving.

If serving is leading you to burnout rather than grace, then it's
a sign that your serving is not an expression of true humility. The
apostle Paul described the attitude and behavior of true humility
to the Philippians:

> Let nothing be done through selfish ambition or conceit,
> but in lowliness of mind let each esteem others better
> than himself. Let each of you look out not only for his
> own interests, but also for the interests of others.
>
> Let this mind be in you which was also in Christ
> Jesus, who . . . made Himself of no reputation, taking
> the form of a bondservant, and coming in the likeness
> of men. And being found in appearance as a man, He
> humbled Himself and became obedient to the point of
> death, even the death of the cross. (2:3–8)

The Lord doesn't say we must not care about our own interests; He says, "Look out *not only* for your own interests." Devalu-
ing our lives is false humility and will not position us to receive the

grace of God. The humility that attracts God's grace into our lives is Jesus's humility, the kind that says, "I'm going to take the greatness on my life and use it to make You great."

THE TEST OF SACRIFICE

Esteeming others as better than ourselves means maintaining a perspective that our life is not about us. Humble service is what connects us to something bigger than us—the kingdom and body of Christ—in which we play a vital part.

I want to see a generation that believes they have a destiny. I long to see the church speaking life over people and calling them to greatness. I am all for building a culture in the church where people are allowed to dream and are empowered to go after those dreams. This is the type of church we want to see established in our city. This is a passion of mine and one I believe we must pursue. But if we aren't careful, those environments can unintentionally lead people to develop an inward focus and think, *It's about my destiny, my dream, my call, and my passion.* These are all good things, but it's vital to keep our destiny and call in the context of outward focus, the context of serving. Otherwise, we can turn inward without realizing it, and our life, call, passion, destiny, and dreams can quickly become all about us.

No passion in our life should be larger than our foundational passion to love, serve, and be obedient to Jesus. Unfortunately, I meet a lot of people whose particular passion to do X, Y, or Z is bigger than their passion to serve the body of Christ or the community in which God has placed them. We become more passionate about pursuing a dream than pursuing Jesus. And that means it's about us.

Recently I sat down with someone in my office and asked him where he was serving.

"I play drums on the worship team," he said.

I said, "I love that you are going after the passion you have to play drums. But that doesn't necessarily mean you are serving. What would you say if the worship leader came to you and said, 'I don't actually need somebody to drum; I need somebody to administrate the schedule'?"

Most people would respond, "I don't feel called to administration." That is where the true test is. What passion is motivating you?

> **If our serving never really requires us to sacrifice for something bigger than ourselves, then it's likely that our serving is about *us*.** ✍

Often we don't realize that what we are doing is actually about us. I went on to challenge the drummer that his call was bigger than his passion for drumming. And as long as he was only willing to serve the worship team as a drummer, his serving was actually more about him.

It's not that we can't do the things we are passionate about, but doing those things doesn't necessarily mean we are laying our lives down for others.

If our serving never really requires us to sacrifice for something bigger than ourselves, then it's likely that our serving is about *us*. Our serving needs to be about Christ and His body, and the safest way to make sure that we are not living for ourselves is to make sure there is an element of sacrifice somewhere in our serving.

FATHERS AND MOTHERS

Jesus constantly modeled this humble "It's not about me" attitude. He said that He had not come to do His own thing but to serve the Father and lay down His life for the sheep. This is how He revealed the heart of the Father to us. If we want to develop into mature leaders, mothers and fathers who reflect the Father's heart, then we must allow Him to put us in situations that teach us "It's not about me."

I've had many experiences that have gently (or not so gently) reminded me that it's not about me. God seems to like to remind me of this. Writing my first book was one of those experiences. It was vulnerable for me to write the book in the first place, because while I felt confident as a speaker, I felt pretty insecure as a writer. I wasn't comfortable with the idea that everything I had been working on for years would be out there on paper and that I'd know if people liked it or not according to whether they bought the book. It was almost as though I had a baby I was not convinced was cute, but I really, really needed people *not* to tell me they thought my baby was ugly. If someone told me my book wasn't any good, I thought it might crush me.

A few days after the book came out, Kris Vallotton, who is a massive voice of encouragement in my life, decided to promote my book during a Sunday-morning service at our church. During the announcements, he held up a copy of my book and said, "Banning wrote a book. It's really good. Who here has read this book?"

An awkward silence fell across the packed sanctuary. Glancing back from where I was sitting on the front row, I didn't see a single raised hand. Mortified, I thought, *Of course no one has read the book! It has only been out for three days!*

Kris, who doesn't give up easily, put the book down and, as if they didn't clap loud enough, said, "Let's try this again. Who has read the book?"

Of course, nobody had read the book in the last thirty seconds, so nobody raised a hand. I knew people were thinking the book must be terrible since no one had read it.

Shortly after this, I was in England for a Jesus Culture conference. During one of the announcement times, we handed out free copies of our worship CDs. People were rushing the stage, even crawling over one another, to get a free CD.

After we had finished passing out the CDs and people were making their way back to their seats, a staff member began the announcements by holding up my book and saying, "Banning wrote a book about revival. It's really good. You should get it."

Spotting a woman still standing in the middle aisle who had

not received a worship CD, the staff member turned to her and told her she could have the book.

But instead of taking the free book, the woman groaned, "Can I just have a CD?"

I was only fifteen feet away from this woman. I wanted to yell, "I am sitting right here. I have feelings."

I usually have a few "It's not about you" experiences whenever the Jesus Culture Band leads worship at conferences or one-night events. These nights all have the same flow. Kim Walker-Smith and Chris Quilala lead worship with the Jesus Culture Band, I preach, and then we end with more worship. Many times, after the service is over, someone will come up with an excited look on their face.

"What can I do for you?" I'll ask, expecting that they are going to tell me how they have been touched by my message or to ask me to pray for them. Nope. Instead, they will say, "Is there any way you can go get Kim so I can get a picture?"

As much as I don't enjoy humbling experiences, I know the Lord uses them in my life. They not only remind me that this life is not about me, but they give me opportunities to gain more of the Father's heart and prove that my life is truly about Him and His family.

I have to answer the questions:

What am I doing this for?

Is my motivation to be known or to sell books?

Or is it to serve people and see them draw close to Jesus and experience His love?

I want to be a true father who is laying down his life to help those around me thrive, grow, and fulfill their purpose in God.

As a young youth pastor, I used to get irritated when kids from our church would attend another youth group. *Don't you realize we are building something here?* I'd think. I couldn't understand why they would go somewhere else. Then my daughter became a teenager. Before we planted our church in Sacramento, she began attending a youth group at another church. She loved it and was thriving there. I realized I wouldn't care at all if she continued to attend that youth group after we started our church, because I wanted her to be somewhere where she was growing in the Lord and connecting to community. That's all I care about now. I don't care about her coming to our church so our numbers look good. But I did when I was a younger leader.

Similarly, when people visit our church and say, "I don't like this church. I'm going to go somewhere else," I respond genuinely, "Please, go wherever you find God and wherever you're growing."

As a father, that is all I care about. It's not about me; it's about the people God has given me to love and serve.

Joy That Remains

In John 15, right in the midst of telling us to abide in His love by loving and laying down our lives for one another, Jesus said, "These things I have spoken to you, that My joy may remain in you, and that your joy may be full" (verse 11). The joy of Jesus remains in your life and your joy becomes full when you are serving others. This isn't just a nice idea; it's a deep truth you can experience.

In the year we started our church in Sacramento, there were many moments that impacted me greatly. One of those came when I gave a sermon on this subject of serving and laying down our lives for others. At the end of the sermon, I wanted to give our people an opportunity to respond, so I asked all the single mothers to stand. Across the room, single mothers began to stand up. I then announced that we were going to practice what we had just heard about serving by giving money to these moms.

I think single mothers are some of the most amazing people. Their strength and courage are really stunning. So I loved the opportunity for our community to serve the single mothers in our midst.

> **The most joyful people I know are also the greatest servants I know.**

Immediately people got out of their chairs, streamed toward these women, and put cash and checks into their hands. Many stayed to pray a blessing over them. What impacted me was not just seeing many of the single mothers weep as people came to serve them, which was so powerful, but the joy we could feel in the room as people served these ladies in a practical way. It seemed like everyone was grinning from ear to ear as they experienced Jesus's joy in serving.

There's a great lie in our culture that we'll be happiest if we set up our lives solely to take care of our own interests. Many have bought into the scarcity mindset that sees life as too full, too fast paced, and too overwhelming to think about someone else. But a mindset defined by selfishness and the fear of lack cannot lead to joy or happiness; it only leads to more restlessness and dissatisfaction. The Bible gives us a great secret to happiness when it tells us to look out for the interests of others as well as our own. Serving positions us for the reward of joy—the same reward that Jesus Himself pursued when He endured the cross (see Hebrews 12:2).

The most joyful people I know are also the greatest servants I know.

PLACE OF SAFETY

Serving is also a place of safety simply because we avoid stepping into spiritual danger zones whenever we align ourselves with Jesus and do what He is doing. The safest place we can be in life is alongside Jesus, doing what He is doing. And what is Jesus doing? Scripture tells us twice that Jesus is continually making intercession for us before the Father (see Romans 8:34; Hebrews 7:25). Jesus didn't stop serving us when He ascended to heaven. He is still serving His body, and that means that serving His body is the place of safety for us.

Having kids has taught me all kinds of lessons about safety. When my daughter Raya was born, it didn't take SeaJay and me very long to figure out that we were dealing with a very different child than our first daughter, Elli. Elli was laid back. She didn't crawl until ten months, didn't walk until fifteen months, and never tried to open a door or a cabinet. Raya, on the other hand, wanted to open everything. I had to put latches on every cabinet and door and even a special lock on the front door because she kept opening the door and walking off. We wouldn't notice she was missing until a neighbor would bring her back and ask us, "Is this your child?"

One week after Raya turned two, she and SeaJay were in the upstairs master bedroom. SeaJay went into the hallway for a second, and when she turned around, the door was closed. When she tried the knob, she found it was locked. She called for Raya but heard nothing. After thirty seconds of silence—thirty seconds was all it took for Raya to get into trouble—SeaJay went into worst-case-scenario mode. She wasn't sure what to do, so she called my dad (I was away on a trip).

"She's locked in our bedroom," SeaJay explained to Dad. "What should I do?"

My dad, a retired police officer, didn't hesitate: "Kick the door down."

"What?" SeaJay asked, not sure she had heard him correctly.

"Kick the door down," he repeated. He then proceeded to give her a quick tutorial on how to kick a door down.

SeaJay hung up the phone, stepped back, took a deep breath, and kicked in the door to our bedroom just as Dad had instructed.

There was Raya, sitting on the floor with a big smile on her face and wondering what all the fuss was about.

I will never forget coming home and finding a busted door-frame and a door split in half and hanging on its hinges. I laughed when SeaJay told me the story. There was no way she was going to be kept from her daughter. SeaJay knew the safest place for Raya at that age was right next to her.

We may not be two years old, but the same applies to us. The safest place we can be is right next to Jesus.

> **The safest place we can be is right next to Jesus.** ✒

Only when we position ourselves to do what He's doing, think what He's thinking, and walk with Him are we safe—and that means taking His posture of serving.

More Can Hurt Us

One of the ways serving protects us is by positioning us so that when God adds increased blessing, responsibility, and influence to our lives, it doesn't crush us. Remember, the purpose of blessing is to enable us to serve more effectively. When we ask for a financial increase, it must not be merely so that our needs are met but so that we can be more generous in serving. When we ask for strength, grace, or favor, it must be so that we can empower and give grace to others.

If we don't know this, we will use our increased blessings to make our lives more about us, which will only hurt us. I've seen people pray for financial increase, and when they had more money, it didn't help them but instead hurt them. I've seen people in ministry who increased in anointing and favor, but because their hearts were not positioned to serve more effectively with what they got, it actually hurt them in the end. I believe many people are not walking in all that God has for them, because it would hurt them if He released it to them. They haven't positioned their lives alongside Jesus, who didn't come to *be* served but *to* serve.

OUR JOB, HIS JOB

Serving, as an act of humility, positions us for what the Bible calls "being exalted," which means receiving honor and being promoted to greater levels of authority, responsibility, and influence. Some believers are uncomfortable with the idea of being exalted, because they know that exalting themselves is a dangerous trap. Jesus was clear in telling us that self-exaltation would only lead to humiliation:

> So He told a parable to those who were invited, when
> He noted how they chose the best places, saying to them:
> "When you are invited by anyone to a wedding feast, do
> not sit down in the best place, lest one more honorable
> than you be invited by him; and he who invited you and
> him come and say to you, 'Give place to this man,' and
> then you begin with shame to take the lowest place. But
> when you are invited, go and sit down in the lowest place,
> so that when he who invited you comes he may say to you,
> 'Friend, go up higher.' Then you will have glory in the

presence of those who sit at the table with you. For whoever exalts himself will be humbled, and he who humbles himself will be exalted." (Luke 14:7–11)

While it's true that self-exaltation leads to demotion, it is equally true that we have another option. If we humble ourselves, exaltation will come from God. Exalting ourselves is destructive because we're trying to do what only God can do.

> **Exalting ourselves is destructive because we're trying to do what only God can do.** ✒

God clearly tells us that exalting us is His job. After Peter quoted Proverbs 3:34—"God resists the proud, but gives grace to the humble"—he said, "Therefore humble yourselves under the mighty hand of God, that He may exalt you in due time" (1 Peter 5:5–6). Our job is to humble ourselves, to take the low road. God's job is to exalt us, to expand our position of visibility and influence; and it's a job He wants to do. He tells us we are the light of the world, and He wants to add grace to our lives so we can shine brightly. He tells us how to do our job so He can do His.

FAITHFULNESS WITH WHAT IS ANOTHER'S

Consider how serving positioned Moses so that God could exalt and release him into his calling and destiny. We know that Moses had a sense of destiny on his life by the time he was forty, because he was stirred to kill an Egyptian he witnessed oppressing a fellow Hebrew. Yet God did not release Moses into his destiny until forty years later, when Moses was eighty. At this point Moses was doing something very different from wandering around and looking for wrongs to right:

> Now Moses was tending the flock of Jethro his father-in-law, the priest of Midian. And he led the flock to the back of the desert, and came to Horeb, the mountain of God. And the Angel of the LORD appeared to him in a flame of fire from the midst of a bush. (Exodus 3:1–2)

Moses received his call in the context of caring for his father-in-law's sheep. He received his own flock—the people of Israel—while he was taking care of somebody else's flock. This was no coincidence. It's how God works. Here's how Jesus described the logic behind God's way of entrusting us with more:

> He who is faithful in what is least is faithful also in much; and he who is unjust in what is least is unjust also in much. Therefore if you have not been faithful in the unrighteous mammon, who will commit to your trust the true riches? And if you have not been faithful in what is another man's, who will give you what is your own? (Luke 16:10–12)

If you want to position yourself for God to advance you in your calling and increase your capacity to manage greater responsibility and resources, Jesus said, then your serving needs to go beyond random acts of generosity and humility. You need to serve as a faithful steward of that which belongs to somebody else.

People often ask how they can get a vision for their life. My first answer is, "Serve somebody else's vision." It isn't the only way to get vision, but it's one of the best ways. Similarly, if you want the Lord to increase your finances, anointing, or some other resource in your life, ask Him to give you an opportunity to be entrusted with those things on behalf of someone else. The Lord wants to release to you what's yours, but He wants to know if you're going to be faithful with what He gives you, so He gives you opportunities to be faithful with what belongs to someone else. If you can be faithful with what belongs to another person, you can be entrusted with what is yours.

THE ENDGAME

In the parable of the minas, Jesus told the story of a nobleman who received a kingdom and then wanted to find suitable people to appoint to positions of authority. His strategy was to entrust a few servants with some money to manage for a time. Later, he called the servants to account for how they had used his money. The servants who successfully invested the money were promoted to rule over cities and regions of various sizes. The one servant who refused to invest what the king had entrusted to him was stripped of his position and possessions (see Luke 19:12–26).

The message of this parable isn't complicated, but it is sobering. Jesus, our King, is looking for men and women who can rule and reign with Him. He wants to find faithful servants, those whom He can promote, who can handle the responsibility of sharing His power and authority. And the test He will use to determine who fits the bill is stewardship—being faithful with what belongs to another.

> **God's calling on our lives is bigger than we can imagine. It goes beyond this life and into eternity.** ✍

God's calling on our lives is bigger than we can imagine. It goes beyond this life and into eternity. He wants to give us a place of honor, authority, and leadership in His eternal kingdom. In light of our eternal destiny, almost everything we get caught up in pursuing in this life—the things we perceive as measures of success and happiness—fade into nothing. We have to learn to position our lives for eternity and to celebrate the things that lead to eternal success.

At Jesus Culture, we have an opportunity to focus on and celebrate eternal success over and above temporal success every time we release a worship album. Every album we put out shows up on a chart that measures its sales from day to day and week to week. For us, as it is with most worship leaders, creating the album was never about sales but about bringing a gift to God and praying it will ignite a deeper love for Jesus in the hearts of people. But we still watch the charts to see how an album is doing, and it can be encouraging to see that people are buying the album. Ultimately, however, sales and charts are not what make us happy.

When one of our Jesus Culture artists, Derek Johnson, released his first solo worship album, it hit the number one spot on the Christian charts on iTunes. While I was encouraged to see Derek's album at number one, I had a deeper excitement for him. On the day his album hit number one, I posted this thought on Instagram:

> I love seeing Derek Johnson on the top of the charts today.
> Not because charts mean anything, because they don't. In
> five years, the place you had on a chart won't matter, let
> alone eternity. But I'm happy to see the worship that was
> developed in the secret place impact the world and ignite a
> fire in the hearts of people. What matters in life is obedi-
> ence and loving well. I'm stoked to see Derek at #1 today
> but even more stoked that I've seen Derek for years go
> after what matters, wholehearted obedience and loving
> God passionately and loving people well.

I dream of seeing a generation of mature leaders overflowing with the grace and joy Jesus promised to those who lay their lives down. Our world is crying out for servants who can handle the weight of blessing and influence, who will use them not only to look after their own interests, but also to humbly and generously invest what they've been given to strengthen and build those around them.

The soil of serving is one of the richest places to grow your roots. It is there they can grow deep and wide and can get the nutrients they need to bear lasting, impactful fruit.

Soil 3

COMMUNITY

11

When Fish Swim Alone

As for the saints who are on the earth,
"They are the excellent ones, in whom
is all my delight."

Psalm 16:3

God's process in David's life was designed to prepare him to be a leader who could handle the weight of increase and promotion. Along with the soils of intimacy and serving, God planted David in a third soil that contained vital nutrients for his root system: *community*.

> David therefore departed from [Gath] and escaped to the cave of Adullam. So when his brothers and all his father's house heard it, they went down there to him. And everyone who was in distress, everyone who was in debt, and everyone who was discontented gathered to him. So he became captain over them. And there were about four hundred men with him. (1 Samuel 22:1–2)

God gave David a band of misfits to live with and lead. It was in this soil of community that David learned the value and strength that comes through relationships.

The soil of community is absolutely essential to God's process of growth in our lives. As I said in chapter 6, community is the other guardrail, along with Scripture, that keeps us on track while we grow as leaders in the body of Christ and in the world.

FROM COLD TO HOT

Those of us who have grown up in Western culture have a steeper learning curve than other cultures when it comes to the issue of community, because we celebrate individualism. Sarah Lanier, a Youth with a Mission (YWAM) missionary, has a fascinating take on the cultural differences between cold and warm climates. In her book *Foreign to Familiar,** she suggests that cold-climate populations tend to be more individualistic in their thinking and approach to life. Cold-climate cultures, she adds, are generally more task driven and hold as a core value that truth matters more than anything else. In contrast, warm-climate cultures tend to be communal, more relaxed, and have as a core value that relationships matter more than truth.

In her travels as a missionary, Lanier has had to learn to navigate these differences. For example, she was scheduled to fly from northern Europe, a cold-climate culture, to South America, a hot-climate culture. It dawned on her that she needed to get all her

---

* Sarah A. Lanier, *Foreign to Familiar: A Guide to Understanding Hot- and Cold-Climate Cultures* (Hagerstown, MD: McDougal, 2000).

work done while she was in Europe, because once she was in South America, she would need to focus more on the people around her and wouldn't be able to get as much work done. When she arrived in South America, her host family showed her to her room. She noticed there was a mattress on the floor next to her bed, so she asked what it was for. Her hosts explained they would never dream of asking her to stay in a room by herself, so they had asked someone to sleep next to her during her visit. In their culture, privacy means unwanted isolation.

Lanier mentions that in some communal warm-climate cultures, such as among certain African tribes, the people don't have a singular possessive pronoun in their vocabulary. They don't have the words to say "This is *my* guitar." They can only say "This is *our* guitar." Their language reflects their communal thinking.

A missionary from Kenya agreed that the culture there was much more relational. When I asked him to describe the cultural differences, he said, "Everything happens much more slowly in Kenya because of relationships. If there's a fifteen-minute walk to the grocery store, I plan an hour and a half, because in Kenya you would never, ever walk by somebody you know and not stop and talk for fifteen minutes. I once went to the bank, got in line to wait, and after a few minutes everyone in front of me started to step out of the line and walk away. When I asked them why they were leaving, they explained that the person at the front of the line was a friend of the teller and they were catching up. They knew their conversation could take a while, so they decided to come back later."

Those stories are hard for me to wrap my head around as

someone who grew up in a Western, task-driven, individualistic culture. The idea of having a stranger sleep on the floor beside my bed to keep me company doesn't sound comforting at all; it sounds awkward and uncomfortable. And changing my schedule of errands just because some guy wants to chat with his friend at the bank? You've got to be kidding me. There is a time for that, and it's during nonbusiness hours.

But I am aware that community-driven cultures carry a value for community that my culture lacks, and this lack makes it more difficult for us to understand and embrace God's value for community. For those of us steeped in Western individualism, it can be very countercultural for us when the Lord takes us into the cave of community to develop our root system. It seems at times we are swimming upstream. But this soil is crucial if we are to bear the lasting fruit God has called us to bear.

Jesus on Community

As in everything, it's vital that we build our lives on the words and example of Jesus. He is the example we follow and the model upon which we base our lives.

The Gospels make it clear that Jesus lived in community. He and His disciples traveled, ate, slept, and worked together. When Scripture mentions some of the occasions in which Jesus took time away from His disciples to commune with the Father, it not only shows us that He had a secret-place lifestyle, but it implies that Jesus often hung out with His community. Jesus was not a loner. He had real relationships with His disciples—not strictly professional or nonmutual relationships. Yes, Jesus was their leader, but He brought them in close enough to have real intimacy. Jesus and His disciples had arguments, made jokes with one another, and showed affection. Jesus was the kind of leader who invited His best friend, John, to lay his head on His chest at dinner.

Jesus had plenty to say about the value of community and relationships in the kingdom. When we read what He said, it is clear that the message of community is not just the latest fad in the church; it is in the heart of God. Consider what Jesus taught in the Sermon on the Mount: "Therefore if you bring your gift to the altar, and there remember that your brother has something against you, leave your gift there before the altar, and go your way. First be reconciled to your brother, and then come and offer your gift" (Matthew 5:23–24). In other words, Jesus was saying, "If you come to have communion with the Father and realize you're disconnected from a brother in your life, put communion on hold until you get reconnected with your brother." That's how important our connections with one another are to Jesus.

Perhaps Jesus's greatest statement on community is found in His high-priestly prayer in John 17. After giving His final instructions and promises to the disciples at the Last Supper in John 13–16, Jesus closes the meeting with a prayer that distills the deepest, most fundamental desires and priorities on His heart. These were not only His desires and priorities for the disciples but for all those who would follow Him—including you and me:

I do not pray for these alone, but also for those who will
believe in Me through their word; that they all may be
one, as You, Father, are in Me, and I in You; that they also
may be one in Us, that the world may believe that You sent
Me. And the glory which You gave Me I have given them,
that they may be one just as We are one: I in them, and
You in Me; that they may be made perfect in one, and
that the world may know that You have sent Me, and have
loved them as You have loved Me. (17:20–23) ·

Jesus's ultimate goal is that what He taught in John 15—that
we would remain in Him and love one another as He has loved
us—would result in our being *one* with one another as we are *one*
with Him. Jesus is passionate about community and makes that
clear in His teaching and prayer. If we want to honor and follow
Jesus, His passion for community must become our passion for
community.

THE BIG STORY

The passion for community we see in Jesus is, of course, God's
passion for community, and it not only permeates the Gospels but
all of Scripture. However, if we read Scripture through the lens of
Western individualism, we can miss this biblical theme.

In *The Blue Parakeet,** professor Scot McKnight claims that
people approach Scripture in a variety of ways. One of those ways

---

* Scot McKnight, *The Blue Parakeet: Rethinking How You Read the Bible* (Grand
Rapids: Zondervan, 2008).

is to see the Bible as though it's a bunch of puzzle pieces to figure out individually and then put together to form a picture. This approach is off base, McKnight argues, because rather than being pieces of a puzzle, the Bible is actually many stories interacting with one another within one big story. And that big story has a central theme. The Bible, he says, is about *oneness being restored.*

> **The story of Scripture is Creation, Fall, redemption to community, and that community finding redemption in God.** ✍

This story begins with humanity being created in the image of God, and that image meant oneness—oneness with God, oneness with ourselves, oneness with one another, and oneness with the world. When the Fall happened, it brought otherness, that is, the loss of oneness. Because of sin, humanity experienced otherness with God, otherness with ourselves, otherness with one another, and otherness with the world. Jesus came to restore the oneness that was lost through the Fall. The good news of the gospel is not merely that we are forgiven of sin but that Jesus has made us one with Him, with the Father, and with one another. The more we express this oneness in our lives, the more the image of God becomes visible in the people of God.

McKnight points out that when we read the story of the Bible through the lens of Western individualism, we end up thinking that the story is about Creation, Fall, and individual redemption in our personal relationship with God. We miss the truth that the real story is not about the restoration of one relationship but of all relationships. The story of Scripture is Creation, Fall, redemption to community, and that community finding redemption in God.

CHRISTIANITY WORKS IN COMMUNITY

There is a phrase I've heard over the years that has some truth to it, but the truth has been co-opted to support an individualistic view of our relationship with God. The phrase is "You + Jesus = Majority." The original significance of this phrase meant that in moments when you have to stand alone for God, He is with you, and He is greater than any enemy or opponent you may face. But people have come to use it to mean "It's just me and Jesus." While it's entirely true that Jesus's sacrifice was complete and opens the way for you to experience eternity in His presence, it's *not* just you and Jesus. That's not how God set it up. Never once did Jesus say, "It's just you and Me. You don't need anybody else in your life." He's the One you need for salvation, but when you connect with Jesus, He points you toward people and says, "Welcome to the family." A better phrase would be "You and the large family God has placed you in + Jesus = Majority." You were never meant to live life alone. You were meant to live in community.

Jesus repeatedly emphasized that our interactions with other people matter in our relationship with Him. He said, "You can't tell Me you love Me while hating a brother. Your interaction with that person over there is tied to your interaction with Me. Do you want to love Me? Love people."

Independence and isolation may be natural in our culture, but they are countercultural to Christianity. Christianity simply doesn't work in isolation and independence. It only works in the context of community. The apostle Paul illustrated this principle brilliantly by likening the community of believers to the human body:

> The way God designed our bodies is a model for under-
> standing our lives together as a church: every part depen-
> dent on every other part, the parts we mention and the
> parts we don't, the parts we see and the parts we don't.
> If one part hurts, every other part is involved in the hurt,
> and in the healing. If one part flourishes, every other part
> enters into the exuberance.
>
> You are Christ's body—that's who you are! You must
> never forget this. Only as you accept your part of that
> body does your "part" mean anything. (1 Corinthians
> 12:25–27, MSG)

We will never enter into the fullness of who we are in Christ, Paul explained, until we embrace the reality that we are "members of one another" (Romans 12:5), because Christ has made us one in Him.

In his letter to the Ephesians, Paul explicitly said that our growth as believers only happens in the context of community:

> And [Jesus] Himself gave some to be apostles, some
> prophets, some evangelists, and some pastors and teachers,

for the equipping of the saints for the work of ministry, for
the edifying of the body of Christ, till we all come to the
unity of the faith and of the knowledge of the Son of
God, to a perfect man, to the measure of the stature of
the fullness of Christ; that we should no longer be children, tossed to and fro and carried about with every
wind of doctrine, by the trickery of men, in the cunning
craftiness of deceitful plotting, but, speaking the truth
in love, may grow up in all things into Him who is the
head—Christ—from whom the whole body, joined and
knit together by what every joint supplies, according to the
effective working by which every part does its share, causes
growth of the body for the edifying of itself in love.
(4:11–16)

What is it that "every joint supplies"? It's *grace.* In the preced-
ing chapter, we saw that grace comes into our lives as we embrace
humility and service. But if you look at the wider context of Peter's
exhortation for us to humble ourselves so that God's grace would
come into our lives, you'll see that he was not only talking about
humility expressed in service but humility expressed in *relational
submission:* "Yes, *all of you* be submissive to one another, and be
clothed with humility, for 'God resists the proud, but gives grace
to the humble'" (1 Peter 5:5).

If we want to position ourselves to receive God's grace and let
Him exalt us in due time, we must not only serve others; we must
submit to others. Grace flows into our lives as we submit ourselves
to one another in relationships.

A lot of people, including leaders, are trying to live and lead with no grace in their lives, because they won't submit to others. It's actually an expression of pride to refuse to submit our lives to others and to act as though we don't need other people.

This kind of pride is rampant in American culture. We celebrate the so-called self-made millionaire because we love the idea that we can achieve success without anyone's help. When someone says, "I made this money on my own, without the help of one person," we applaud the person because we want it to be true. In our culture, needing other people is often perceived as a sign of weakness and independence is viewed as the true sign of strength.

> **If we want to position ourselves to receive God's grace and let Him exalt us in due time, we must not only serve others; we must *submit* to others.**

This pride isn't just rampant in American culture; it has crept into the church. For example, people are embarrassed to tell me that they see a counselor, because they don't want to admit they need someone else's help. They'll kind of whisper it to me, as though it's a secret: "Hey, I see a counselor." It's as though they expect me to reply, "Wow, that's hard to believe. I didn't know it was that bad. I didn't know you were so messed up you actually had to talk with somebody and ask for help."

We have to accept that we need one another because God designed us that way. Whenever we try to function outside of

God's design, we end up in trouble. Accept the fact that you need others.

Growing up around two lakes, my friends and I learned to drive boats in our teenage years. The first thing you are taught when learning to drive a boat is never to start the boat out of the water. A boat must only be started, not on the dock or in the driveway, but in the water. The reason for this is that a boat engine is designed to sit in the water, draw the water up, and push the water through itself to cool it. If you start the engine out of water, it will quickly overheat.

What a great picture of our life. Christianity is meant to sit in the context of community, for it's in community that we draw the grace needed to do what God has called us to do and to become the person God has called us to become. I talk to so many people who tell me, "I don't know what's going on. My life is just fried." When I probe a little deeper, I find out that they are trying to live life in independence and isolation. I tell them, "You're not living in the context where you can draw the grace you need into your life. You need to get in community."

ISOLATION IS A KILLER

When I was a youth pastor in my early twenties, I didn't really know what I was doing, so I ended up sitting in an office with a lot of time on my hands. This was pretty boring, so I bought a fish tank to make my days a little more interesting. I got a fifty-five-gallon tank from a friend and bought two big fish called severums at a pet store. It only took a few days for me to realize these fish were not going to help my boredom problem. They were the most boring fish I had ever seen. So I went back to the pet store and asked if they had some more exciting fish, perhaps fish that would school together. They showed me a tank filled with tiny colorful fish darting around in a school.

"Those look perfect," I said, "but I have two bigger fish—will they bother these little ones?"

They assured me that my severums would leave the little fish alone, so I bought ten of them and brought them back to my office. As I had hoped, it was much more fascinating to watch these ten colorful fish schooling around. As the days passed, it seemed like the two severums were coexisting peacefully with their new tankmates.

Then one day I noticed that one of the little fish was not swimming with the school. I watched it exploring on its own for a bit, mildly interested, but I didn't think much of it.

When I returned to my office the next day and looked at the fish tank, I couldn't believe it. I counted several times to make sure, but there could be no doubt. I now had two big fish and *nine* little fish.

The next day I noticed that another of the little fish had split off from the group and was swimming on its own. The following day I counted my fish. I had two big fish and *eight* little fish.

A day or two later another little fish began swimming apart from the group. Sure enough, the next morning I had only *seven* little fish. A few days later I had *six*. The pattern continued. One fish at a time wandered off from the school and disappeared, until all ten of the little fish had been eaten by the big fish.

I couldn't help feeling there was a lesson in this fish drama. It seemed significant to me that as long as the little fish stayed together, they survived. Within twenty-four hours of separating from the group, they were dead. The lesson? *Isolation is a killer.*

Nothing destroys the power of shame or offense like choosing to move toward community.

The Enemy will do everything he can to isolate you. He either tries to get you so hurt and offended that you say, "I feel misunderstood. I don't want anybody to control my life. I want to do my own thing." Or he tries to isolate you with shame over some issue in your life. Whenever you find yourself hiding from people or trying to push them away, an alarm bell should go off inside you that says, "The Enemy is trying to isolate me!" Next, you should have the same response every time that alarm bell goes off: "I'm going to go talk to someone. I refuse to be isolated, because isolation is a killer." Nothing destroys the power of shame or offense like choosing to move toward community.

THE HARD CHOICE

I've been on a journey of community for the last twenty years. In my early twenties, I was isolated and independent. I didn't want to be vulnerable with my personal struggles, and I didn't like anybody telling me what to do. So the Lord stuck me in community and made me learn how to do it for eighteen years.

I won't lie; it was hard. It was messy, sticky, draining, slow, and frustrating. But at the end of the day, what I realized is that community just flat-out works. Throughout those eighteen years, I watched a lot of peers in ministry who didn't want to make the hard choice to do community. They didn't want to submit their lives to other people. Today, they're not doing what they are supposed to be doing, because they refused to access the grace they needed to be successful from community.

As much as you have been hurt, frustrated, or annoyed by community, you must make a deliberate choice to stay in it. We do get hurt in community. But we also get healed in community. Community is where we grow. We cannot live without it.

12

It's Messy, but It Works

Behold, how good and pleasant it is
when brothers dwell in unity!

Psalm 133:1, ESV

received a phone call from someone I knew in ministry. She
said, "Banning, I want to give you a heads-up. My husband and
I are getting a divorce."

After a moment of shocked silence, I asked, "So . . . who have
you been talking to about your marriage?"

"Nobody."

"You haven't talked to anybody about your marriage? You
haven't met with anyone about what you are going through?"

"No, we haven't."

She went on to describe some of the issues they had been
struggling with and concluded, "We've tried our best, and it's just
not good enough. It's not working."

When I got off the phone, I couldn't help trying to relate
what she had said about "trying their best" to my own marriage. I

thought, *If I had just tried my best in my marriage, I don't think it would have lasted. I'm not sure we'd be together today if I had just done my best, because my best isn't good enough.*

God doesn't require only my best. If I stand before God and He asks, *What happened to your marriage?* I'm not going to be able to say, "Well, I gave it my best, and it didn't work."

He's going to say, *I didn't require just your best. I required your best, and I required you go to other people in your life and bring their best into your marriage.*

There's not one area of my life that is healthy or fruitful that doesn't have the best of others poured into it. The health in my marriage is because we've given each other our best and because we've gotten the best from people in our community and brought it into our marriage. Anywhere I have fruit in my life—finances, parenting, leadership, or ministry—is an area in which I have sought the wisdom and strength of my community and brought it into my life. Those areas have been touched and greatly influenced by others.

STRENGTH

Proverbs 13:20 says, "He who walks with wise men will be wise." Strength is not found in isolation; it is found in community. It's simply tragic how many people in the body of Christ are failing in some area of their lives because they are trying to figure out everything on their own and missing out on the strength that could be accessed from the people around them.

A friend once explained to me that his family was in a very

tough spot financially. "We're about to lose our home," he admitted.

"How long have you been dealing with financial issues?" I asked.

"Two years."

"Two years? Who have you talked to about it?"

"Well, nobody," he admitted. "We just thought we needed to figure it out on our own."

> **I've found that there's almost nothing in life that we're supposed to figure out on our own.**

My heart was heavy for this family and their situation. I told him, "I've found that there's almost nothing in life that we're supposed to figure out on our own. I certainly haven't tried to figure out money on my own. There are people God has placed in my life who are full of wisdom in the area of finances. They have wise counsel for finances that has come not only through revelation from God but also through years of failures and success. When I come to them and submit my finances to them, their strength in finances becomes my strength. When I disconnect from them, I disconnect from the strength God wants to give me."

When we walk with those who are wise, we gain the strength of the wisdom that is in their lives. We're not supposed to figure things out on our own. When we end up over our heads—which will happen all the time in God's process of growth in our lives—we need to know that the strength, wisdom, and grace God wants to give us are most likely going to come when we humble ourselves and reach out to our community. For this reason, when I get in over my head, I do two things: I get with the Lord, and I immediately call somebody who's farther along than I am and ask, "What do you think? I need your strength and wisdom." Again and again, the wise counsel of my community has helped me navigate the deep end.

SAFETY

Solomon, the wisest man in the Bible besides Jesus, wrote many proverbs about the value of community. One of the things he reiterates is that *safety* is found when we access the wisdom of our community:

> Where there is no counsel, the people fall;
> But in the multitude of counselors there is safety.
>> (Proverbs 11:14)

> Without counsel, plans go awry,
> But in the multitude of counselors they are
>> established. (15:22)

> For by wise counsel you will wage your own war,
> And in a multitude of counselors there is safety.
>> (24:6)

There's a big difference between making decisions on our own and making them in community. According to the book of Proverbs, decisions made "in the multitude of counselors" are safe. Decisions made outside are unsafe. We are called to make decisions in community. The challenge with making decisions in community, however, is that it requires *humility* and *submission*.

It takes humility to ask other people for counsel—humility that perhaps comes easily when you're young and inexperienced but gets harder as you get older and feel pressure to be an expert on things.

As I mentioned in chapter 2, I served as an overseer at a school of ministry for a few years in my early twenties. The only position I had held prior to that was as a youth pastor. Suddenly I was being asked to counsel adults at least twice my age. Many of the students were dealing with deep issues that were far beyond me, and for a long time I felt helpless.

During one session, while attempting to counsel a woman who had been married for years, I realized I had absolutely no idea what I should say. Desperate, I asked the woman, "Can you hold on just a second?" I left the room and sprinted across campus to the office of our church's family pastor and counselor, Danny Silk. I described the woman's situation to him and asked, "What do I do?" After Danny walked me through several steps I could suggest to the woman, I sprinted back to my office where she was patiently waiting, perhaps assuming I had been in the bathroom for a really long time. I then passed on the wisdom Danny had given me, not mentioning I had just gone and borrowed something I hadn't had fifteen minutes earlier.

I can't begin to count how many times in my twenties I ran to my leaders with questions like that. Around the time I turned thirty, I started thinking that I didn't want to ask questions anymore. *Asking questions,* I reasoned, *makes me look like I don't know what I'm doing. Kids ask questions,* I told myself, *not experienced leaders.* But as soon as I became aware of this thought, I made a deliberate choice to continue asking questions, to continue humbling myself and being willing to look like I didn't know what I was doing, because the truth is, I still don't know what I'm doing. I had to resist the pressure that I was supposed to have it all together by age thirty, and I had to hold on to my humility.

Letting Community Set the Pace

Along with the humility to ask for counsel, we must submit to honoring any counsel when we receive it.

For me, one of the biggest areas I have to work on about submission is in allowing my community to test, judge, and weigh in on what I am hearing from God. I have a core value that to make decisions in community, we need to practice hearing the Lord together. Scripture clearly tells us that when we hear the Lord speaking, we ought to share it with others and allow them to judge what we have heard (see 1 Corinthians 14:29). So I have people with whom I share what I am hearing from the Lord and ask, "Tell me what you think. Is this the Lord? Am I hearing this correctly?"

As I have submitted what I was hearing and feeling to the leaders and community in my life, I found that often it wasn't

what I was hearing that was off, but rather the timing I was sens-
ing. As I mentioned before, everything seems too slow to me. And
I definitely did not like to hear someone say to me, "This isn't the
right time for that." I've usually already built a plan around whatever I've heard, and I'm ready to act *now*. So it's tough for me to
submit to others in my life and put on the brakes. But I do so for
two reasons. One, I see lots of people who refuse to submit to
other believers what they think they are hearing from God, who
instead do things on their own and make unsafe decision after
unsafe decision. Two, somebody early on told me that one of the
big tests in my life would be whether or not I would rush to get
ahead of the Lord. I've found that community is the thing that
keeps me from rushing ahead.

Again and again I've found what Solomon said to be true,
that the decisions I make in community are safe, but the ones I
make in isolation end up being unsafe.

I'm not saying it's easy to adjust my pace to walk in community, because in my mind, community is slow. I always feel we
should be going faster than we are. But over and over I have found
that when I allow my community to set the pace for my decisions,
I end up with the right timing for whatever God is doing.

GOD'S VOICE

Scripture is clear that God speaks through people. As I mentioned
earlier, He obviously speaks through Scripture, and He speaks to
us personally. But God also speaks through people, and that
means God speaks through community. So when we disconnect

from community, we are disconnecting from one of the ways God speaks to us.

Occasionally people will tell me, "God is being silent to me right now."

I will challenge them about that. "God is not being silent to you," I will say. "He's just speaking through somebody you're not connected with."

Very often God puts His voice in somebody's life and then requires you to be in relationship with that person to hear Him. The hard part is that every person God speaks through is imperfect. This fact threw me off for a while. I wanted God to speak only through those who had perfect character, great attitudes, phenomenal communication skills, and all the right information. But the Lord doesn't do that. The message often comes through a messenger who is not that qualified (in my opinion).

There was a season in my life when I had really hard conversations with three people, two outside my church and one inside, within a month or so. Each of these people took hold of me and went after me with a laundry list of issues. Most of it was incorrect and based on misinformation, and all of it, I felt, was delivered with the wrong attitude. The problem was that, as I listened to them, I could hear the Lord in some of what they were saying.

This really irritated me. I went back to the Lord and said, *God, I don't like how these people are coming at me. I think they're wrong in a lot of areas. So why is it that I can hear You speaking in some of what they're saying? Why are You speaking to me through these rough packages?*

In essence, the Lord told me, *Banning, I'm giving you a chance*

to humble yourself and hear My voice through other people or to
dismiss everything because you don't like how it's being delivered.

It's amazing how many times we dismiss the voice of God because we don't like the imperfect person He is speaking through. We have to be able to hear people, even when they're not completely correct and may come with the wrong attitude. The truth is that none of us is perfect, and none of us knows how to communicate perfectly. We all grew up in different environments. If you grew up in a conflict-avoidance environment, you learned to hold things in until you couldn't hold them anymore. Then after you blew up, you went back to holding everything in. In other homes, lack of conflict means you don't care about the relationship. In community, especially in marriage, we discover that the different communication styles we learned are all flawed and easily misunderstood. This is why humility is essential to community and why we must be able to listen well.

BLIND SPOTS

The book of Proverbs is filled with words like *reproof, rebuke,* and *instruction.* Every time, the ability to listen and receive these things in your life leads to wisdom. The inability to receive them is foolishness. Receiving feedback and correction is absolutely essential if we want to keep growing. The moment we stop receiving feedback is the moment we start to stagnate and die. One of the best ways to grow is to listen to feedback from those around you.

Many of us have a hard time listening to feedback. The

moment someone tells us what they see going on in our lives, we get defensive, stop listening, and start building a case of excuses or counterarguments:

- "You have a bad attitude."
- "You don't have all the information."
- "I won't listen to you while you're hurting. I'll only listen if you have no emotions when you speak to me."
- "If you had more information, you would come to the same conclusion I've come to, so I'm going to overload you with some more information."

If your first reaction to feedback is defensive, dismissive, or diminishing, you need to stop for a second. Resistance to feedback means there's a good chance you're not aware of, much less checking, your *blind spots.*

> **Receiving feedback and correction is absolutely essential if we want to keep growing.**

One of the only car wrecks I've had in my life occurred when I was driving through South Central Los Angeles at the age of eighteen. While I was in college, I would go down to LA about twice a month and serve with a ministry that did sidewalk Sunday school for children. It was a powerful time for me to see God touch people's lives, and I grew to love those kids. One time when my parents came to visit, I wanted to show them the neighborhoods where we ministered to these incredible children. As I was driving in the big-city traffic of Los Angeles, which was like nothing I had encountered in the small city I grew up in, I looked in my mirror, but I didn't turn my head to look over my shoulder at my blind spot before I started to change lanes. Suddenly I saw there was a car right where I was trying to go, so I swerved back into my lane—only to end up rear-ending the car in front of me.

We all have blind spots. God has not given us a 360-degree view of our lives. But it's not only God who reveals the areas we must see. Do you know who else can see our blind spots? *Community.* People in our lives can see what we can't see, and we need to be humble enough to listen when they tell us what they see.

> **People in our lives can see what we can't see, and we need to be humble enough to listen when they tell us what they see.**

I'm not saying every person in your life gets a level of access to bring correction or input to your life. The people you listen to on a regular basis should be trustworthy. But I am saying that you *must* have people in your inner circle checking your blind spots and letting you know what they're seeing.

As a young leader, I observed Christians who loved the Lord, heard clearly from Him in certain areas, and were spiritually gifted, yet they were not making great decisions in their lives. I noticed that most of these people seemed isolated and lacked healthy relationships with other believers. But why should that be a problem, I thought, when these people ought to be able to hear directly from God about their issues? I was confused by this and went to a spiritual father and asked, "Why doesn't the Lord speak to these people and say, *Stop acting the way you are acting, please*?"

He said, "God doesn't bypass discipleship just because we don't want to be in it." He then explained that God instructs all of us to have relationships with people who can speak into our lives and challenge us and encourage us, that is, practice discipleship. We can't live isolated lives and expect God to speak to us apart from people. If we do not set up our lives to listen to those around us, we will miss out on something God is trying to tell us.

You can hear God in a profound way in many areas of your life, but there are some areas where He will only speak through community. Just because you don't like that setup doesn't mean God will bypass it to talk to you in that area.

COURAGE

One of the main battles Christians face is discouragement. The Enemy knows it's going to take a massive amount of courage to do what God has called us to do and to become the people God has called us to become. If you look at the areas of your life where you deal most with discouragement, it's likely these are key areas connected to your calling and purpose in God.

I'm convinced more and more that we have in the church a

huge deficit of courage that we keep trying to fill with more information and teaching. I want to tell people, "You don't need more teaching; you just need the courage to do what God has called you to do."

> **You don't need more teaching; you just need the courage to do what God has called you to do.** ✍

Courage is something you have to go after. It will not come to you. You must set up your life to be encouraged, and one of the main ways courage comes into your life is through community. It's not the only way, but it is one of the main ways. Throughout Scripture we see pivotal moments in which one person instills courage in another and enables that person to fulfill a God assignment. Before Joshua leads Israel into the Promised Land, God comes to Moses and says, "But command Joshua, and encourage him and strengthen him" (Deuteronomy 3:28). Paul encouraged individual leaders, such as Timothy, and the churches he oversaw. To the Romans, Paul said, "For I long to see you . . . that I may be encouraged together with you by the mutual faith both of you and me" (1:11–12). Community is where we find courage.

The story of Esther is probably one of the most profound stories of courage in the Bible. So often we zoom in on her brave declaration, "If I perish, I perish" (4:16), and imagine she reached that moment on her own. But that's not how the story goes. The

story of Esther is also about Mordecai, her cousin who adopted
her as a daughter and fathered her through the process of becoming a candidate for queen of Persia. When he learned that the Jews
were about to be slaughtered, Mordecai confronted Esther with
the mandate on her life:

> [Mordecai] also gave [Hathach] a copy of the written
> decree for [the Jews'] destruction, which was given at
> Shushan, that he might show it to Esther and explain it
> to her, and that he might command her to go in to the
> king to make supplication to him and plead before him
> for her people. (4:8)

Esther's initial reaction to this message from Mordecai was
not "All right, I'll do it. I'll go talk to the king." Instead, she said,
"If I go before the king without being summoned, I'll die" (see
verse 11). Mordecai responded with a statement that ends with
one of our favorite phrases: "for such a time as this" (verse 14). Yet,
like Esther's statement of bravery, we often forget to keep Mordecai's words in context:

> And Mordecai told [the messengers] to answer Esther:
> "Do not think in your heart that you will escape in the
> king's palace any more than all the other Jews. For if
> you remain completely silent at this time, relief and
> deliverance will arise for the Jews from another place,
> but you and your father's house will perish. Yet who

knows whether you have come to the kingdom for such
a time as this?" (verses 13–14)

Mordecai did not let Esther off the hook. He held her to the
hard choice before her and said, "This is it. Do something or die.
What if this is your destiny?" He called her to courage. Only after
Mordecai confronted her did Esther find the courage to do what
she needed to do. There would have been no Esther without Mordecai. She didn't have the courage necessary to fulfill the call of
God on her life without him.

> **When you disconnect
> from community, you
> disconnect yourself
> from a massive source
> of courage that you
> will need for what God
> has called you to do.**

We need this kind of encouragement in our lives. God calls us
to do impossible things. Some of these impossible things are the
battles on the inside over character issues that seem insurmount-
able. We feel powerless to overcome weakness in ourselves, much
less stand up to enemies outside us. This is why we need people to
speak courage into our life, who say, "You have what it takes. You
can do what God has called you to do. You can become who God
has called you to become. We're here with you, praying with you."

When you disconnect from community, you disconnect yourself from a massive source of courage that you will need for what God has called you to do. Esther found the courage she needed because she was connected to community. Joshua, David, Ruth, Timothy, and countless others found the courage they needed when they were connected to community. Community is where you'll find the courage you need too.

COVERING

Acts 13:1–4 tells us of Saul (Paul) and Barnabas being sent out on their first missionary journey:

> Now in the church that was at Antioch there were certain prophets and teachers: Barnabas, Simeon who was called Niger, Lucius of Cyrene, Manaen who had been brought up with Herod the tetrarch, and Saul. As they ministered to the Lord and fasted, the Holy Spirit said, "Now separate to Me Barnabas and Saul for the work to which I have called them." Then, having fasted and prayed, and laid hands on them, they sent them away.
>
> So, being sent out by the Holy Spirit, they went down to Seleucia, and from there they sailed to Cyprus.

Paul encountered God in many dramatic ways and wrote much of the New Testament. He had a relationship with Jesus. You might think that the Holy Spirit would send Paul out by speaking to him in a dream or vision. Instead, the sending came through community. The church at Antioch fasted and prayed, laid hands on Paul and Barnabas, and sent them. But the very next phrase says, "So, being sent out by the Holy Spirit . . ." The Holy Spirit sent Paul and Barnabas out through community.

When I meet with young leaders, one of the things I am most interested in finding out is "Who sent you? Whom are you under? Who can tell you no? Who can pull back your reins? Who has input in your life, not because they give you a paycheck, but because you've asked them to give you input?" If they can't tell me who sent them, then, in my mind, they're not safe.

The Holy Spirit hasn't changed the way He works. He intends to call, empower, and send us into the world as witnesses to the gospel through community. He releases His voice, His grace, His protection, and His courage to us through community. Our root system simply will not grow strong and sustain lasting fruitfulness unless our roots are deeply planted and drawing life from community.

Rooted in the Source

For the earth shall be full of the
knowledge of the LORD
As the waters cover the sea.

And in that day there shall be a Root
of Jesse,
Who shall stand as a banner to the
people;
For the Gentiles shall seek Him,
And His resting place shall be glorious.

Isaiah 11:9–10

S aul and David were both chosen and anointed to be king of
Israel. They each reigned for the same amount of time, about
forty years. Both achieved significant victories and successes, and
both made some huge mistakes. Yet the fruit these two men left
behind could not be more different.

Saul is remembered as the king who was rejected and cut off

by God, the king who tried to do things his way and attempted to kill his God-appointed successor. David, on the other hand, is remembered as the king after God's heart, the king who prized God's presence, always repented of his sin, and not only passed the baton successfully to his son Solomon but ultimately became the ancestor and "father" of the Messiah. For eternity, the resurrected Christ is called the Son of David and sits on the throne of David. It's hard to comprehend the magnitude and significance of such a legacy. God has forever attached Himself to the name of a man who lived thousands of years ago. That's fruit that lasts.

The critical difference between Saul and David lay in their root systems. Saul was never planted in the soils of intimacy, serving, and community as David was. Above all, he was never connected in a deep, abiding way to the *source* David had in his life. What was that source? It was Christ! In the book of Revelation, Jesus told John, "I am the Root and the Offspring of David" (22:16). The New Living Translation puts it this way: "I am both the source of David and the heir to his throne." David was rooted in Christ and thus produced the fruit that lasts, namely, Christ.

If the fruit of David's life had come through some other source, his legacy would have no bearing on our lives. He would be another ancient king in history. But David's source is our source. But more than that, we have two things David never had. We have Christ's superior example of how to be rooted in the soils of intimacy, serving, and community, and we have a deeper and richer connection to Christ, our source, because of the finished work of the cross.

David had intimacy with God—more intimacy in some ways than many of us have. Yet he only glimpsed the kind of intimacy Christ makes available to us: the intimacy of walking with God in friendship and partnership and being filled with His Spirit.

Likewise, David experienced the benefits of serving and identified himself as the Lord's servant till the end. Yet Christ demonstrated an even fuller life rooted in the soil of serving. He not only served the Father as a faithful servant, but He did so as a faithful Son, and He showed us that in that relationship, there can be no greater *joy* in life than serving.

Last, we see many clear examples where David, both before and during his reign, was strengthened, counseled, and supported by the community around him. Yet our experience of community in Christ is even more dynamic, because Christ Himself lives in each member of His family and His grace flows to and through us as we lay down our lives for one another.

So what kind of legacy do you want to have? You are chosen and appointed to bear fruit that lasts for eternity, just like David, just like Christ. But it's your choice to *remain* in Christ. Will you let Him teach you to trust Him at all times, even in weakness? Will you let Him plant you where He wants you, and will you embrace His time line for establishing your roots? Will you put your roots down deep in the soils of intimacy, serving, and community? Every day you get to choose between human success and God's success, between the temporal and the eternal, between the way of Saul and the way of David. It is my fervent prayer that you will choose to be one who is rooted in the Source.

Acknowledgments

As with most things in my life, this book would not have happened without some amazing people who brought their strength to the process. Writing a book is time consuming and means a lot of people cover me.

To Zack Curry, Sheri Silk, and the entire Jesus Culture team, thank you for allowing me to disappear for a season to tackle this project. I can't imagine doing this journey without all of you.

To Allison Armerding, thank you for bringing not only your literary talents but your heart and passion for the message in this book.

To Nathan Edwardson, Becky Johnson, and Dean Deguara, thank you for helping me shape the content and the communication of that content.

To Darren Lau, Skyler Smith, and Cody Williams, thank you for being cooler than I am and making what I do look good.

To Brock Shinen, thank you for displaying your belief in me and in Jesus Culture by the way you selflessly lay down your life.

To Esther Fedorkevich, I could not have done this without you in my corner.

To the entire WaterBrook Multnomah team, your strength and belief in this book was felt immediately. Thank you for helping me expand what was on my heart. It's been a joy to work with you.

To Bethel Church and the entire leadership team there, thank you for creating an environment where valuing the process pushed me to a place where my life became rooted in God's Word, God's presence, and God's family.

To SeaJay, Ellianna, Raya, and Lake, thank you for your grace during the season of my writing this book. Your lives constantly reveal the goodness of God to me, and I would not be here today if it weren't for each one of you.